A LIFE IN M(

SCOTTISH FOOD AND [DRINK] MEMORIES

HELEN WELSH

Best Wishes,
Helen Welsh

the porridge press

ISBN: paperback 978-1-9162418-0-0

ISBN: ebook 978-1-9162418-1-7

FOREWORD

A number of years ago, reeling from life's events, I spent three whole days in a library. The kind of library where you officially eat and sleep as well as browsing around the shelves. I read about a method of telling your own story. Not that I expected anyone to be remotely interested in reading it. (Let's hope I was wrong about that.) But it seemed to me then, in my battered and bruised state, that writing my story could be a great triumph. Finding things to say about myself which might help me feel that I wasn't a total eejit who had wasted every good opportunity that had come my way. I think it worked; at least something has worked because here I am again, restored and with much the same gall as before.

Here's the method:

1. Divide your life into five-year packages (so if, for example, like me at the time of writing you're in your early sixties, you will have 13 packages to consider.)
2. For each of those packages, think of a memory that was vivid, exciting, fun, terrifying, tragic, wonderful or whatever. Think deeply and remember accurately. Be selective. Probably not the day you learned to cast off your own knitting. But maybe the day you trounced the school bully in the inter-school spelling bee? Or the day your paper aeroplane penetrated the Rings of Saturn – with you attached, at the end of a long string?
3. Write each of the stories. Put them end to end. Voila! YOUR LIFE. Full of good and exciting things in which you are the hero. The master/mistress of your own fate. The captain of your own soul. Thank you, William Ernest Henley ('Invictus' – see overleaf).

I have chosen a grand buffet of food and drink stories to illustrate my five-year packages. I have always loved food and drink – and last year when I revisited this method and started writing the packages in earnest, I had just finished a Master's degree in Food and Drink Innovation; so food and drink were very much on my mind. It's an embarrassing thing to admit that most of your waking thoughts centre around what you're going to put in your mouth next; but, hey – I know I am not alone.

Although I have written lots of fiction in my time, this book is non-fiction. In other words, the places and characters are real, and the events described really happened. Apart from the bits where I embroidered, re-imagined, or used heavy doses of artistic licence! Some names have been changed to prevent me being sued. Fingers crossed. And the original 13 chapters had to be split up a bit.

If you too are obsessed by food and drink; or if you like Scotland, where I have grown up and lived for all but the first two years of my life; or if you like to read about how 'real' people get by in life without the trappings of wealth or connections or celebrity status: then you might enjoy this book. I hope you will; I have certainly enjoyed writing it.

INVICTUS

Out of the night that covers me
Black as the pit from pole to pole
I thank whatever gods may be
For my unconquerable soul.

In the fell clutch of circumstance,
I have not winced nor cried aloud.
Under the bludgeonings of chance,
My head is bloody, but unbowed.

Beyond this place of wrath and tears,
Looms but the Horror of the shade.
And yet the menace of the years
Finds, and shall find, me unafraid.

It matters not how strait the gate
How charged with punishments the scroll
I am the master of my fate:
I am the captain of my soul.

— W.E. HENLEY (1875)

(The title 'Invictus' was used by Clint Eastwood in his acclaimed 2009 film, developed from the book 'Playing the Enemy: Nelson Mandela and the Game that Made a Nation' by John Carlin. It tells the story of the 1995 rugby world cup, hosted by South Africa. Nelson Mandela (played by Morgan Freeman) was aware that, post-apartheid, South African citizens were still divided racially and economically – and also in their attitude to rugby, which was seen as a white man's game. So he joined forces with the Springboks' captain, Francois Pienaar (played by Matt Damon), to promote unity through the universal popularity of sport. The Springboks were not expected to win, as this event marked their return to the championship after being excluded on the basis of their apartheid history. However, with Mandela's magnetic statesmanship, the game turned out to be thrilling, emotional and decisive. The story as portrayed in the film was held to be accurate, in a context where it was thought to be impossible to achieve such unity; and the film enjoyed critical and commercial success.)

CONTENTS

PROLOGUE: SAUSAGE SANDWICHES

My first food memory was a sausage sandwich. I was four years old at the time, and in the kitchen with both my parents. This in itself was unusual, because one of them had left home before my memories began. Here's the story, as I remember it.

I lived with my Mum and my older brother Roddy in a tied cottage in the Ayrshire countryside, next to Auchinleck Estate. 'Tied' meant that the house was included as part of my mother's wages, for heavy domestic and dairy work. Ours was the middle of three houses surrounded by fields, cows, a fluctuating pond, and the Glasgow-to-Carlisle railway line. There were children next door but they, along with Roddy, all went to school during the day and I had nobody to play with. So I mooched about around home-time, waiting for them to appear on the road up from the railway bridge, when I would be allowed to run down and meet them. School was in Catrine, a mile and a half away, along twisty stony roads. The bridge was my outer frontier. On this afternoon of my first memory, I was balancing on a pile of logs in front of our cottage, all my attention focused on the distant railway bridge, straining for company.

Someone appeared: but it wasn't Roddy, or the big girls next door.

An old man was walking up the road leaning on a stick, wearing a long brown coat and a soft grey hat, and I recognised him immediately, from photos. I raced in our back door and shouted out, 'Mum! Mum! Dad's coming up the road!'

'WHAT?!' She dropped the potato she'd been peeling. She ran out front and when she saw I'd got it right, rushed back into the kitchen and went stouring around in circles. I couldn't figure out what was going on, so I asked, 'where's he been?'

A tricky question apparently; she stopped in her tracks and snapped, 'he's just been for a haircut!' So, five minutes later the man with the two-year haircut arrived at our kitchen door, carrying a pound of sausages. I was more than curious, I was agog. This was all new. A father in the house? Whatever next? Soon I was sitting on the stranger's knee, bouncing up and down and firing questions. 'Careful!' said this man who appeared to be my father, 'don't tumble!'

'What's *tumble*?' I asked, not recognising the word.

'Stop showing off!' hissed my mother and made me get down and sit at the table. She had heated the dripping in our ever-ready frying pan, and cooked the peace-offering, slathering them into buttered slices from a plain loaf. I'd never tasted anything so delicious. Well, I'd never tasted anything at all before, as far as my memory goes, but there must have been plenty stuff had passed my lips in four years of life. Sausage sandwiches, though – hot and greasy and savoury; I loved them.

By the time my brother got home from school, I suppose it was a cosy domestic scene. The rest of that day's events have not lodged in my brain, but Roddy has told me since that our father found us by figuring out the local school; the headmaster had arrived unexpectedly in Primary 6's afternoon spelling class and announced to all the pupils, 'Roddy McCulloch, there's a man in my office who claims to be your father. Will you please come and verify this.'

The next morning, the postie brought a letter from my sister Mae. 'Dear Mum, just to warn you, Dad turned up in the pub last night when I was cleaning tables and made me tell him where you are. It was embarrassing, he looked like a tramp. Just in case he tries to find you ...'

That's all. These stories are about what I remember first-hand, not what I have come to understand as the years go by. And I'm focusing on the food, because it's such a delicious thing to remember and write about – and more appetising than some of the other memories. And because I'm so lucky that, despite being skint for long stretches of my life, I have never ever gone hungry.

I would like this book to become an airport blockbuster so that I could buy all the sausages in the world and give them to all the children whose fathers have disappeared. And to all the mothers who try to eke things out with dignity. And to celebrate everyday triumphs over clanging adversities. May we thrive and prosper.

THE PERFECT SAUSAGE SANDWICH:
SOME OPTIONS

NOWADAYS I'D CHOOSE A ROLL INSTEAD OF BREAD, BECAUSE THE SAUSAGES WOULD BE LESS LIKELY TO ESCAPE. A SOFTISH ROLL – WHITE WOULD BE TRADITIONAL BUT A NOT-OVERLY-RUSTIC BROWN IS GOOD.

YOU MIGHT PREFER TO CUT DOWN A BIT ON THE GREASINESS OF MY 1960 ORIGINAL – NOT SO MUCH FOR FLAVOUR BUT IN DEFERENCE TO YOUR ARTERIES. THERE ARE VARIOUS WAYS TO ACHIEVE THIS BUT I WOULDN'T GO OVERBOARD:

- LOW-FAT SAUSAGES ARE A POSSIBILITY BUT I'M NOT A BIG FAN. EXCEPT MAYBE FOR VENISON SAUSAGES WHICH ARE NATURALLY LEAN AND VERY TASTY

- YOU COULD FRY IN A LIGHTER OIL AND FORGET THE DRIPPING; OR BETTER STILL, GRILL THEM – SOME OF THE FAT WILL DRIP OUT BUT YOU'LL STILL GET GOOD FLAVOUR

- DO YOU NEED BUTTER TO COMPLETE YOUR TASTEBUD EXPERIENCE? YOU COULD TRY MISSING OUT THE BUTTER, AND MAKE SURE THERE'S PLENTY MUSTARD ON THE ROLL INSTEAD.

Many Scots prefer square, or 'Lorne' sausage — the same sausage meat but made in a loaf tin and cut in slices by the butcher. They are less likely to escape from the sandwich, but personally I prefer good old links. You can slice them in half, longways, to keep them in place a bit.

- *Lettuce and tomato? If you must. It would be unconventional; but why not?*

- *Broon Sauce — HP traditionally — is a frequent adornment. The fruity acidity cuts the grease a bit and complements the fatty meatiness very satisfactorily. But it's easy to overdo. I prefer mustard but then my working-class credentials are long-gone. Choose your own poison.*

CHAPTER 1: SAGO

My sister Mae was something of a mystery figure to me, though she wrote frequent letters and visited when she could afford the bus fares from Birmingham. She had knitted me a jumper for starting school. It was dark green with yellow knobbly bits and my mum had laughed when it arrived, exclaiming, 'Kippers and Custard!' This was her and Mae's joke for the uniform of Bartley Green Grammar School, which Mae had attended in previous years. Voluminous dark green gym knickers and a hat with a ribbon; a gym slip and a tie. It was a family legend.

When I was six Mae was twenty, lost to me in the mists of adult-hood. She got married in London in June 1963, about six weeks after my father died. She and her fiancé, Neil, had driven up shortly before the time of his death; I remember sharing my bed with her and waking up one morning to find my mother on her knees by the bed, weeping. 'Dad's died,' Mae said, in response to my query. Neil, a policeman, had checked his breath with a mirror. This was mysterious to me but of course nobody wanted to explain it. A pair of tall clothes-horses appeared in our front room, draped with sheets, screening off the bed recess; and I was warned not to look behind them. It occurred to me that my father might be hiding behind the sheets and I was a bit nervous about peeking; but when I did, all I saw was a long wooden box, which was disappointingly dull after all my adrenalin. On the day of the funeral – another mystery to me: what was a funeral and why wasn't I allowed to go, even though I was being kept off school for the occasion? – I was taken to a nearby farm run by the son and daughter-in-law of our neighbours, and spent the day playing with a kitten and being fed on thick soup. The kitchen floor had tiles and I was allowed to play peevers, or hopscotch as you might know it.

I couldn't say I missed my father – my only memories of him were those two years after the haircut – and during that time we barely had any conversation. He just sat by the fire smoking his pipe. I believe he was a bit of an invalid. However, I was alive to my mother's distress and it was all a bit strange for a while.

Nonetheless, life at home seemed to take on a steadier rhythm. Mum, Roddy and I had moved to a nearby village – Ochiltree. On the day of the move, corned beef sandwiches were prepared and I got hold of the key from the tin. Bored as usual, I practiced my figure 8s on the dining-room table. So my first day in Ochiltree was memorable partly for the telling-off I got when my mother caught me at it.

It seems that back then, the Council had a policy whereby only widows could get school-dinner-lady jobs; so, suddenly, my mother was eligible just as a vacancy arose. She also cleaned at a farm in the mornings; and in the run-up to Christmas there was a turkey-plucking job at another farm, a mile out of Ochiltree in the other direction.

Meantime I had started school and throve, being quick at reading. Roddy was taken in hand by the local minister, who was an Army Cadet Padre, and went off to Ayr once a week with his well-blancoed puttees and shiny badges. By this time Roddy was at high school, and his life seemed odd and remote to me. I puddled along happily enough; swinging on the garden gate and drawing pictures in the margins of Mae's old Sunday School prize copy of AA Milne's 'When We Were Very Young', and any other books I could lay my hands on. We didn't have other paper, what was the problem? When Mae found out, her displeasure was considerable and shortly thereafter, I found myself without anything else to draw on.

I think my sago memory must have been around my seventh or eighth year. It involved my sister, and the farm outside Ochiltree where my mother worked. Mae must have come up for a few days to visit us, without Neil. I guess my mother, proud of her smart and pretty eldest daughter, doing well for herself Down South, made her come with us to the farm one summer's morning when there was no school.

We used to get the ten past eight bus to the Mote Toll and start walking from there – about a mile to the farm. Sometimes we were picked up by car if it suited the farmer's other jobs for the day. In my memory, my sister only ever wore dainty little shoes with heels, so walking a mile must have been a bother.

It was a dairy farm, and the working day started about 4am with the milking. So by the time we arrived it was already well into the working day. Mum's jobs here were all domestic – no outside heavy cleaning of dairy dishes, but plenty hard and constant slog, keeping a farmhouse clean and tidy and its occupants fed and watered. The farm was run by a mother and son – Mrs T, the matriarch, and her silent son Bill, then in his forties perhaps. They both worked hard and Mrs T was the Boss, and I was well warned about politeness and doing as I was told and not getting in the way and making myself useful. And, because my mother was proud and stubborn, never ever accepting any kind of gift from anyone, especially not money but not even a sweetie. So I dusted and swept and peeled tatties from an early age, but when Mrs T, to everyone's astonishment, tried to give me ten shillings for my forthcoming holidays (two weeks at Mae and Neil's), I resisted firmly and was not to be persuaded. I don't know how my mother got round that one but I think Mrs T gave her the money to spend on me. There may have been an ice cream.

That's all just context. This particular day, Mum and Mae and I arrived at the farm and set about the routines. I guess Mae must have been given a duster too because nobody got to hang about doing nothing. We always had 'the ten o'clock' – milky coffee, scones and chocolate biscuits – then dinner at 12 noon. Dinner was three courses and preparing it was my mother's job. Always soup, of the brothy variety; tatties with sausages or mince and turnip or carrots or cabbage; and some kind of pudding. Then tea in a white china cup and saucer. Then Mrs T would have a siesta and I was warned to keep quiet.

The puddings varied and were often steamed – jam or golden syrup in the bottom of the basin with the sponge batter poured on top, sealed off with greaseproof paper and string, and the whole thing set to steam for a couple of hours, then turned out and served with custard. They were sweet and surprisingly light; my absolute favourite was the one with golden syrup.

These big lunches were very filling and kept us going all day, so my mother didn't have to feed us too heartily later on. Fodder, you might say; good solid stodge, functional and enjoyable enough. Except for the sublime steamed puddings.

On this day, however, Mrs T had something else in mind for pudding: sago. Sago? I had never heard of it; it wasn't in my mother's usual repertoire. I was intrigued. I did my clattering around with the peeling of the tatties and the setting of the table – for five, that day; Mrs T and Bill, Mum and Mae and me. As always, it was 'speak only when spoken to,' and I was well used to quietly, politely and efficiently putting away my dinner. But

Mae wasn't; and it was a bit awkward trying to figure out what Mrs T, Bill, or indeed my mother would make of her bright conversational assays. Not my problem thank goodness, nothing I was expected to fix, so I just kept eating, with one eye on Mum, waiting for the inevitable sharp reprimand to sail in Mae's direction. It didn't come.

Soup plates cleared to the sink; dinner plates away. Time for pudding. Up came the sago. I peered at the pot, puzzled. White with shiny globules – not very enticing. I took a little on the edge of my spoon and lipped it off. The flavour wasn't bad, just not very evident. I took a spoonful in my mouth and discovered the globules didn't melt as I worked them round my mouth. Squeezing them up into my palate with a rigid tongue. They stayed globule. I cast an eye at my mother for guidance, and found a glare that said, 'don't you dare.' So I breathed in through my nose and swallowed. Down went the globules, whole. Slithering one by one down my throat. I breathed out and blinked. I was alive! But there was still a bowlful of the stuff in front of me – another dozen spoonfuls, I estimated. Another glance at Mum – slitty eyes and the silent message, 'get on with it.' Oh boy, it was like Cabbage Wars back home; but I knew better than take my mother on in front of other people, especially the Boss. So I had to do that thing with your brain where you think of something completely different to try to trick yourself into not noticing the gag-inducing stuff you are ingesting. I imagined myself up the braes gathering rosehips, for which we would be paid 3d a pound at school come the autumn.

Thus engaged, I was oblivious to anyone else's response to sago; until Mae's polite, English accent cut through my fog. 'No thank you,' were her exact words. A little gasp all round the table, and I'm sure my eyes were as big as my open mouth. *No thank you?* What on earth? Was the world going to end? I could scarcely bear my mother's shame. But then as was frequently the case, I had underestimated her unassailable pomp when faced with disaster. Swift as a gazelle she scooped up my sister's bowl and spooned the offending mass into mine. Tidying up to throw it all out? Of course not, how could such a thought even cross my mind? 'Helen will eat it,' she announced, smiling sweetly.

And so this is Helen, human dustbin and saviour of the family face.

STEAMED PUDDING

(IF YOU WANT INSTRUCTIONS FOR SAGO, LOOK ONLINE. I COULDN'T TAKE THE RESPONSIBILITY.)

NOBODY STEAMS A PUDDING NOWADAYS – EXCEPT MAYBE A CLOOTIE DUMPLING ONCE IN A WHILE, FOR A SPECIAL OCCASION. IT TAKES SO LONG. BUT IF YOU FEEL CURIOUS ABOUT IT, YOU MIGHT GIVE IT A TRY. A PRESSURE COOKER CUTS DOWN ENORMOUSLY ON THE COOKING TIME, BUT NOBODY HAS PRESSURE COOKERS NOWADAYS EITHER. THERE ARE MICROWAVE VERSIONS BUT I DON'T LIKE THEM – THE FLAVOURS DON'T GET A CHANCE TO DEVELOP, IN MY VIEW, AND THE SPONGE ISN'T SO GOOD, AND YOU DON'T GET THE NICE EFFECT AS YOU PLOP THE BOWL UPSIDE DOWN AND THE SYRUP OR JAM CASCADES DOWN THE SIDES OF THE PUDDING.

BEFORE MICROWAVES WERE INVENTED, SPONGE PUDDINGS IN TINS ARRIVED IN THE SHOPS. MY MOTHER TUTTED AT THE LAZINESS OF IT, BUT OTHER PEOPLE SAID THEY WERE QUICK AND EASY.

IN ITS DAY, THE STEAMED PUDDING HAD SOME GREAT VIRTUES – (A) IT WAS CHEAP TO PRODUCE, AND (B) IT WAS FILLING, ESPECIALLY WITH CUSTARD. NOBODY CARED ABOUT CALORIES; KEEPING THE FAMILY FED AND HAPPY, WITHIN A TIGHT BUDGET, WAS THE THING.

INSTRUCTIONS:

GREASE A SMALL BOWL WITH BUTTER AND PUT SOMETHING IN THE BOTTOM OF IT FOR FLAVOUR — NOT TOO MUCH — IT COULD BE A TABLE-SPOON OR SO OF JAM OR SYRUP, OR MAYBE A CHOPPED-UP COOKING APPLE. THEN MAKE A BATTER — I'D SETTLE FOR THE EASY ALL-IN-ONE SPONGE VARIETY, WITH 2 EGGS, AND 4 OZ EACH OF SELF-RAISING FLOUR, CASTER SUGAR AND BUTTER, ALL CREAMED TOGETHER. YOU COULD ADD A TEASPOON OF CINNAMON OR GROUND GINGER IF IT SUITS YOUR CHOSEN BOTTOM-OF-BOWL FLAVOURING. AND IF YOU WANT TO BE DECADENT YOU COULD ADD A TABLESPOON OF COCOA TO YOUR SPONGE MIX.

SPOON THE BATTER ON TOP OF YOUR JAM OR WHATEVER — YOU WANT THE MIXTURE TO COME TO ABOUT HALF AN INCH OFF THE RIM OF THE BOWL. THEN GET SOME GREASEPROOF PAPER AND DOUBLE IT; MAKE A PLEAT IN THE TOP TO ALLOW FOR EXPANSION; AND TIE IT ONTO THE TOP OF THE BOWL WITH STRING. THIS IS REALLY A TWO-WOMAN JOB, OR A WOMAN-AND-CHILD JOB — YOU NEED A SPARE FINGER TO HOLD THE STRING WHILE YOU KNOT IT. TIE IT SO THAT YOU GET A STRING HANDLE ACROSS THE BOWL, FOR LIFTING IT OUT AFTERWARDS.

GET A BIG PAN GOING ON THE STOVE WITH AN INCH OR SO OF WATER BOILING IN THE BASE. ADD AN UPSIDE-DOWN PLATE TO ACT AS A TRIVET, TO RAISE YOUR PUDDING ABOVE THE FLOOR OF THE PAN. LOWER YOUR BOWL IN CAREFULLY AND COVER THE PAN TIGHTLY. KEEP IT AT A SIMMER, AND CHECK FROM TIME TO TIME THAT THE WATER LEVEL HASN'T GONE DOWN TOO FAR; LET IT COOK FOR 2 HOURS.

LIFT IT OUT WITH TONGS OR A WOODEN SPOON OR SOME OTHER IMPLE-MENT TO AVOID BURNING YOURSELF; CUT OFF THE STRING, PEEL OFF THE PAPER, AND — THIS IS THE GOOD BIT — TURN IT UPSIDE DOWN ONTO A WARMED PLATE. IT LOOKS AND SMELLS LIKE GRANNIE'S HIELAN' HAME. SLICE AND SERVE WITH CUSTARD OR CREAM.

CHAPTER 2: BROWN TROUT

We had a fork in our cutlery drawer with a hole punched in the handle, and the letters NAAFI stamped underneath. When setting the table, it was 'Mum's fork'. She had worked in a NAAFI canteen during the war, and still had her old cookbook complete with annotations. I have since learned that you could be called up to work in the NAAFI – Navy, Army and Airforce Institute – and I have an old photo of my mum in NAAFI uniform, but I don't know whether she was military or civvy. I always just presumed it was a job like any other; my ignorance.

Despite reports I've read since, of lumpy gravy and other culinary undesirables, I was proud that my mother had been a cook in a NAAFI canteen. It was certainly a formative experience for her. She was 23 when war broke out; having started her working life in 1930 'in service', at the age of 14, carrying out domestic work for wealthy families in big houses. The scholarship she had won to attend Hamilton Academy was out of reach because her father – Highland gardener-turned-miner – couldn't afford for her to stay at school. She recalled wearing a blue dress in the morning for cleaning, and a black dress in the afternoon for answering the door and conveying visitors to the lady of the house. She felt well-treated by her employers and wasn't bitter about her lowly position – why would she be? The work was mainly indoors, and she was praised for being well-spoken and attentive as well as hard-working. But she reminisced often about the precious gems she had encountered in school – Latin, French, and Mathematics. *'Amo, amas, amat ...'* she would say; 'the square on the hypotenuse of the right-angled triangle ...'

In any case, I'm guessing that working in the NAAFI as part of the war effort must have been exciting and rewarding at least in part – no doubt exhausting, dirty and heavy too; but that would have been the common experience of all men and women sent to war. Food rationing posed a bleak challenge and along with tens of thousands of other women, she vigorously set about beating it. Wasting food meant going hungry – how wretched, and how reminiscent of the experiences of the General Strike in 1926, when she remembered carrying her school soup down to the playground railings for her striking brothers to devour. Also, as the propaganda machine reminded her and her compatriots daily, wasting food meant losing the war on the home front. How could they be so derelict when their fathers and husbands and brothers and sons were overseas facing mortal danger? It was out of the question.

For us at home, then, we were always skint – more than skint, actually quite poverty stricken. 'Do we know any poor people?' I remember asking my mother one day when I was about nine, having been subjected to a long rambling talk on poverty at school assembly. She looked at me in disbelief. 'We ARE the poor!' she replied. I was aghast. Surely not?

In any case, we never, ever went hungry. My mother had the skills and the wit to ensure that we always went out with full bellies. School dinners helped, as there were always leftovers even after she had urged them on all the hungry children. Back then school dinners were excellent, at least in my memory, and a blind eye was turned to the final destination of food not consumed on school premises. So, throughout my childhood, I had free school dinners twice a day – mutton stew, cold thick-sliced ham or pork or roast beef with salad and chips, thick mince, mashed tatties to turn into tattie scones with a bit of flour and margarine. We did a little gentle foraging – mushrooms when we knew of a place, and of course gooseberries and brambles. And she was always making soup; there were plenty eggs through the farm jobs; plenty fry-ups; a chip pan full of lard lived on the stove-top. She grew some veg in the garden so we had tatties, carrots, onions and strawberries. Occasionally she would come home from the farm with an old hen. I would come in from Amo-amas-amat to find her at the kitchen sink, up to her elbows in feathers and chicken guts. The stink could be fearsome, and I was especially unkeen on the appearance of inner eggs which hadn't yet grown a shell, spilling out into the basin. But of course it was transformed in the cooking into a wonderfully tasty feast, and back then, as far as I was aware, eColi and salmonella hadn't been invented. I certainly don't ever remember stomach upsets. We were stoic appreciators of good food; or, if the 'goodness' of the food available was in question, at least we would appreciate that it was filling and tasty.

Sugar and flour were plentiful and cheap, and like most of the women of her acquaintance, especially in the farming community, my mother was a competent baker. When I was about twelve, she showed me how to make shortbread and by some stroke of luck it turned out well; so I got to repeat it. Scones, pancakes, sponges, chocolate cake, buns, tarts – they all got churned out on a regular basis and it was a social disgrace to offer anyone a bought biscuit or cake along with their tea when they called in unannounced.

My mother had a good grip of Scotland – that is to say, she was a stout wee woman; and I have become a stout, taller woman in later life. Her stoutness was testament to her determination to thrive through hard times. My own excuses are probably less convincing.

As I was growing up, I spent a lot of time with my friend Marian. She came to Ochiltree when she was nine and I was eight, and lived less than a mile away at Langholm Farm, which was managed by her father. When she was going to school or anywhere else she used to leave her wellies at our house, the first at the bottom of the village, to get changed into clean shoes. And I spent a lot of time on the farm, playing at schools in the attic, and helping her mum with wee jobs as required. Her mum, Mrs Mitchell (at that time we always addressed adults by their titles – it would have been unthinkable to call them anything else) regularly invited me to stay for tea.

Marian's mum was much more than a good cook; she was an artist. Maybe ten years younger than my own mother, she was full of energy and adventure, and vigorously debated the issues of the day ('women equal to men? Away wi' that – women are far superior!') while dishing out jobs for us to do. My first memory of having tea at Marian's is of brown trout from the burn, beautifully set out on china plates at a table set with country charm. A whole fish, on a plate with new potatoes and a tomato, just for me! And everyone round the table with the same, and the story of the fishing of it being offered around with relish. And I was even invited – actually, expected – to join in the conversation!

In our teens, Mrs Mitchell sent Marian and me up the braes to collect sloes, and then had us sit and prick holes in them with a pin before she steeped them in gin. By that time, Marian and I had a nice gin-and-bitter-lemon routine going on whenever there was a young farmers' dance – or any other occasion. We used to buy two gins from the bar, with one small bottle of Schweppes bitter lemon. The bitter lemon seemed expensive, so we made it last between us for three rounds. We found it delightful; but it paled beside the revelation of home-made sloe gin, which Mrs Mitchell gave us to taste. My mother probably never knew I drank gin, and would doubtless have been horrified. But it was such a delicious, enticing thing to learn about the magic you can work in a kitchen.

I learned loads from Mrs Mitchell as the years went by – not just specific skills and knowledge about cooking, but about elegance in simplicity; generosity even in hard times; commitment to high standards and the skills needed to achieve them; good conversation at table; and having a bit of fun along the way.

TO MAKE SLOE GIN

SLOES ARE LITTLE HARD BLUE-BLACK BERRIES WHICH GROW ON THE BLACKTHORN TREE. THEY ARE BITTER AND NOT GOOD TO EAT RAW; BUT STEEPED WITH GIN AND SUGAR THEY CREATE A BEAUTIFUL RED, FRUITY, SCENTED LIQUOR WHICH YOU CAN DRINK NEAT, OR WITH AN ICE CUBE; OR MAKE INTO A LONG DRINK WITH TONIC, JUST LIKE NORMAL GIN.

YOU NEED 500G OF SLOES, 250G OF CASTER SUGAR, AND A LITRE OF GIN – NOTHING FANCY, I USE CO-OP OWN-BRAND. TO RELEASE THE FLAVOUR, THE SLOES NEED TO BE PRICKED, INDIVIDUALLY, WITH A NEEDLE. THIS IS A BIT BORING; IF YOU WANT TO AVOID THIS STEP, YOU CAN PUT YOUR FRESHLY-GATHERED SLOES IN THE FREEZER FOR A DAY OR TWO AS THIS TENDERISES THE SKIN ON THE LITTLE BERRIES, AND THERE IS NO NEED TO PRICK.

PUT YOUR THREE INGREDIENTS IN A LARGE BOTTLE OR A LARGE JAR WITH A GOOD LID, AND GENTLY SHAKE TO HELP THE SUGAR DISSOLVE. STORE IN A COOL, DARK PLACE AND SHAKE A COUPLE OF TIMES A DAY UNTIL THE SUGAR HAS FULLY DISSOLVED, THEN SHAKE OCCASIONALLY IF AND WHEN YOU REMEMBER. LEAVE IT FOR A COUPLE OF MONTHS TO LET THE FLAVOUR DEVELOP. STRAIN THROUGH A MUSLIN CLOTH INTO A STERILISED BOTTLE.

TO MAKE SLOE GIN

YOUR AUTUMN-PICKED SLOES WILL GIVE YOU BEAUTIFUL SCARLET SLOE GIN IN TIME FOR CHRISTMAS.

CHAPTER 3: FREEDOM, MELBA TOAST & THE WHOLE COD

My mother's oft-proclaimed mantra was, 'stick in at the school and you'll no have to work as hard as yer auld mother.' Covertly, she also harboured an alternative life theory: that finding a good man was the best a girl could do to achieve security. Obviously this wasn't derived from her own life experiences, but I guess she lived in hope. As I worked my way through school, doing okay in terms of exam results, and started going out with boys, her anxieties bubbled up a bit. On the eve of my departure for university, she invited a boyfriend I'd recently 'chucked' to come for tea; after all, she reasoned, he was a tradesman (a turner – I'd never heard of such a thing – it was something to do with engineering and therefore, in my mother's view, a job for life, which meant I'd never go without). She clearly thought she might get us back together again and, who knows, prevent me 'having to' leave home. It was excruciating, and must have been for him too. Sorry, Jimmy, if you're reading this. I couldn't wait to get away.

Marian had already been away for a year, in Edinburgh with the Civil Service, having a great time up to a point. Great social life but boring workplace, she being the only member of her team under the – unimaginably ancient – age of forty. However, she had a bedsit and was loving living in her own space, in her own way, away from parental control. That's what I wanted too; it was so tiresome always having to account for everything. And more than that, I wanted away to a bigger world with more possibilities and adventures to be had. The most obvious way for me to achieve this was to go to University, which would be acceptable to my mother and for which I would easily achieve the necessary Highers. So that was the plan.

In my last summer holidays before starting at University, Marian and I went on a cycling trip, over the sea to Skye. It was an odyssey really; practising freedom. Reminiscing with Marian recently, I discovered that her chief memory of the planning was that my Mum insisted we had every night's accommodation booked up in advance – very challenging, pre-Internet – whereas hers was quite happy for us to find beds for the night as we went along. One way or another, by writing loads of letters and sending self-addressed envelopes, we found places to stay – youth hostels in Skye, B&Bs in the Uists. No sleeping on the beach required; at least not overnight.

We got the train to Glasgow, hired bikes, and took them on the train to Mallaig, across the Glenfinnan viaduct, bound for the ferry to Broadford. Everything about that trip was drenched with significance: the rucksack choice (unwieldy blue canvas with tan leather straps, walking boots dangling by their laces), the book I read on the train ('The Vital Spark' by Neil Munro), the merriment I caused Marian by mistaking ferns in a gully by the railtrack for carrots, the iconic Scottish scenery (rugged and far too hilly for bikes), the weather (70% wet), the arguments we had (Marian's wet socks on my bed; me running out of cash, again, far away from any post office for the redeeming of postal orders) – and the food we ate.

I introduced Marian to Wall's pork pies, on a hill above Uig, waiting in a sudden blaze of sunshine for the ferry to

Lochmaddy. In a B&B in North Uist, our landlady gave us a white, jellyish substance, and challenged us to guess what it was. I hadn't a clue; Marian guessed junket, which her mother had occasionally made. But it was Carageen Moss, a sort of milk pudding set with seaweed gathered off the rocks by our landlady herself, or so she said and why would she lie? Exotica. We drank Tallisker, the local single malt, and it felt salty and tantalising. We bought whatever was available in the local shops – biscuits, crisps, sausages, pork pies, tins of this or that – and fed ourselves whenever we were staying in youth hostels. When youth hostels were unavailable (throughout Uist) we ate wherever we could find a meal.

In Lochmaddy there was only one restaurant, rather posh by our standards. It didn't open till 7pm and we were queuing at the door from 6.45, starving. They let us in, gave us the menus, took our orders and those of a couple of other tablesworth of guests, and delivered plates of melba toast – thin, curled-up slices of toasted white bread, very elegant. Mrs Mitchell would have approved. Then the electricity went off. The people at the next table took pity on us in the candlelight, and gave us their melba toast to keep us going till heat and light were restored and the meal continued. I think the meal was all good but the only bit I really remember is the melba toast. Very fancy. Not very filling. But so sophisticated! And such kind neighbours.

Glasgow University student life was wide ranging and very exciting. I learned in Sociology that a tiny proportion of children from benefit backgrounds (me) or single-parent families (me again) got to University, and that most students had attended private school (obviously not me). This didn't trouble me; although I was surprised to discover that I wasn't very good at studying and had mistaken my patchy originality for academic prowess. Still, I got by, more or less. By the skin of my teeth.

In my first year I stayed in a YWCA hostel in Park Circus –

cooked breakfast and two-course dinner provided, bedrooms shared. Hotwater bottles filled at 10pm. The only thing I remember about the meals there was that I was always hungry. This might not be the fault of the YWCA but throughout my first year at University, I ate a cooked lunch in the refectory – something along the lines of pie, beans and chips – every single day, then had the YWCA dinner at night. And if we'd been out somewhere – at a concert or a play, or just for a change, the library – we often bought a steak pie supper on the way home. I ran on stodge, and was a fit size twelve with no health problems. Nowadays those dietary habits seem horrific, but back then it just felt normal, in fact necessary. The faintest whiff of hunger had to be staunched.

I visited Marian in Edinburgh and we went to a concert, then a disco, got terribly drunk, and spent most of the next day slumping around the Botanic Gardens, sleeping on benches among the Henry Moores. However before all that, we were well set up by a meal she had prepared in her little kitchen. 'Mexican Macaroni' was a pasta dish with peas and frankfurter sausages from a jar, the recipe taken from Margeurite Patten's 'Perfect Cookery', which Mrs Mitchell had given her when she left home. She had set the table carefully with colourful tablemats bought from a sale in a shop in Marchmont Road. I was charmed, and wanted all this for myself.

In my second year I moved into a bedsit in Dennistoun, miles away from Uni but it was the only place I could find in my price range. I had a single room in a rundown villa in Circus Drive; possibly the only female lodger and definitely the only student. The landlord was Pakistani and his family lived downstairs; they kept very much to themselves. I didn't see many other tenants, but I became friends with one, a man around forty who lived in the room opposite. He told me he was a compulsive gambler, something I'd never come across before, and that gambling had ruined his marriage as well as his financial situation. He introduced me to tinned tomatoes and the making of Bolognese sauce. Spaghetti, I discovered, didn't just come in tins. You could buy an 18-inch-long purple paper packet, the last word in style; you had to hold the long strands up while they softened and slumped into your boiling salty water.

I entertained (one at a time, no more seats). Katharine Whitehorn had written the perfect book for me: 'Cooking in a Bedsitter'. It addressed the challenges of water and drainage only being available from the bathroom on the landing; doing everything in one pot on one gas ring, and how to manage it all if you were cooking the delightful spaghetti which ideally needed two pots and rings. She had a recipe involving cod (Mediterranean Fish, page 95), and there was a good fishmonger down in Duke Street. So with a visitor pending, I called in one Saturday morning. The queue was out the door with women in headscarves and message bags on their arms, so I had plenty time to look around as I waited. 'Can I have a cod, please,' I asked when my turn came. The fishmonger didn't spring into action to fetch my order.

'A cod?' I wasn't sure if he was looking at me funny, because he had a severe squint in one eye.

'Yes please.'

'Dae ye want a fillet or a steak?' This threw me a bit. I had to get him to explain ('What's a fillet? What's a steak?') because, I said, I thought my recipe called for a whole fish. 'How many are ye feedin?' he asked.

'Just two of us.'

The fishmonger addressed the queue at large: 'Here's a lassie havin a great perty the night,' he announced. 'A hale cod!' There was a bit of tittering and eventually I emerged, a little flustered, with two beautiful cod steaks. Cod steaks! Pearly with pinky edges, bound in their own sparkly-grey vellum, smelling just of themselves and the North Atlantic, double-wrapped in grease-proof. My message basket felt like it was nestling a pair of Fabergé eggs. How was I to know that cod was a big fish? It didn't matter, I would know next time. So I went home to rein-terpret Katharine Whitehorn for cod steaks. With parsley and lemon, oh how exciting it all was. School dinners no more.

I imagine my (private school) guests found a teatime visit to my bedsit a fairly exotic experience, though for different reasons to mine. My cooking equipment was rudimentary though effi-ciently deployed, and I guess they'd never eaten before in a place with all the appurtenances of three rooms crammed in together – a double bed, a gas ring, and a tiny table. One armchair pushed up to the table while I would sit on the bed. They seemed to like it well enough, and kept coming, despite the unfortunate occa-sion of the jobbie in the bath, when presumably one of the other elusive tenants had mistaken the bath for the toilet pan. I didn't know whether to go and complain to the landlord, or clean it up first. We talked it over, my guest and I, and I decided to leave it and hope it would just go away of its own accord – which, even-tually, it did.

I found another inspiring cookbook in a shop in Great Western Road – the 'Friends of the Earth Cookbook'. This was 1975 and I was unaware of FoE as a campaigning organisation; but I learned some lovely things in that book, some of which I still intend trying out forty-odd years later – like, cooking in a hay box. Or rather, finishing off the cooking of a dish by burying it in a box of hay or other insulating material – to save on fuel. It was from this book that I discovered pesto, never heard of back then, made with walnuts and parsley rather than basil and pine nuts, and so good! Especially on the exotic purple-packet spaghetti. Also 'spiced split pea pate,' which has evolved popularly as hummus but again not known back then, and which I still make regularly.

Marian was planning to leave the civil service and Edinburgh and go to France as an au pair, and I merrily planned my first trip abroad, aged 19, to visit her. Meantime, with cod and parsley and lemons and walnuts and split peas and garlic and chillis, I was in clover.

PULSE PATE

YOU CAN USE ANY PULSES BUT MY FoE COOKBOOK SPECIFIED SPLIT PEAS, WHICH CAN BE EITHER GREEN OR YELLOW. YOU DON'T NEED MEASUREMENTS. BUY A PACKET OF DRIED SPLIT PEAS (OR WHATEVER PULSE YOU FANCY) AND PUT SOME — AT LEAST A MUGFUL — IN A BOWL. COVER WITH DOUBLE THE DEPTH OF COLD WATER AND LEAVE THEM OVERNIGHT SO THAT THEY SWELL UP (ACTUALLY WITH SPLIT PEAS IT DOESN'T TAKE THIS LONG — A FEW HOURS WILL DO THE TRICK. BUT IF YOU HAVE CHOSEN WHOLE BEANS OR CHICKPEAS YOU NEED THE LONGER SOAKING TIME).

DRAIN, PUT IN A SAUCEPAN WITH MORE WATER, BRING TO THE BOIL WITHOUT SALTING, AND SIMMER FOR A WHILE UNTIL THE PULSES ARE SOFT. SPLIT PEAS ONLY TAKE 30 MINUTES; MAKE SURE YOU DON'T OVERDO IT. DRAIN AND MASH, THEN ADD A GOOD DOSE OF OLIVE OIL AND PLENTY CRUSHED GARLIC, A LITTLE SALT, THE JUICE OF A LEMON, AND A PINCH OF DRIED CHILLI FLAKES. GIVE IT A GOOD STIR. YOU WANT IT TO HAVE ENOUGH OIL TO MAKE IT SMOOTH AND CREAMY — IF YOU DON'T USE ENOUGH IT GOES DRY, CHALKY AND STIFF. IT'LL STIFFEN UP ANYWAY IF YOU LEAVE IT FOR A FEW DAYS, SO BETTER TO START OFF NICE AND LOOSE.

USE TO SPREAD ON SANDWICHES OR AS A DIP FOR CRUDITES AND

CRISPS. IT KEEPS VERY WELL SO LONG AS YOU KEEP IT COVERED, BUT DOES DRY OUT A BIT AS TIME GOES ON, ESPECIALLY IF YOU HAVE BEEN STINGY WITH THE OIL. YOU CAN CUSTOMISE IT BY ADDING HERBS AND SPICES AS YOU CHOOSE. YOU CAN NEVER GO WRONG WITH PARSLEY.

WESTO (WHAT I CALL PESTO MADE WITH WALNUTS AND PARSLEY INSTEAD OF PINE NUTS AND BASIL):

YOU NEED A BAG OF SHELLED WALNUTS, A COUPLE OF CLOVES OF GARLIC, SOME OLIVE OR RAPESEED OIL, A BIG BUNCH OF PARSLEY, AND SOME STRONG, SHARP, HARD CHEESE – NOT TOO MUCH AND IT'S NOT A DISASTER IF YOU DON'T HAVE ANY – BUT IT DOES FINISH IT OFF NICELY. (YOU WILL NOTICE I'M NOT GIVING QUANTITIES – YOU NEED TO JUDGE THIS FOR YOURSELF, WHICH WILL GIVE YOU FAR BETTER RESULTS THAN IF I GO PEDANTIC AND YOU GET ALL STRESSED ABOUT THE ODD 10G HERE OR THERE.)

IF YOU HAVE A FOOD PROCESSOR, BUNG IT ALL IN AND GIVE IT A WHIZZ. IF YOU DON'T HAVE A FOOD PROCESSOR, YOU NEED TO DEAL WITH IT AS FOLLOWS:

WALNUTS IN A POLY BAG – BASH WITH ROLLING PIN OR OTHER HEAVY BLUNT OBJECT TO A RUBBLE

PARSLEY AND GARLIC – CHOP FINELY

CHEESE – GRATE FINELY

EVEN WITHOUT A FOOD PROCESSOR, IT'S A QUICK JOB. PUT IT ALL IN A BIG BOWL AND MIX/MASH THOROUGHLY. STIR IN OIL TILL IT'S SOFT BUT NOT TOO LIQUID. TASTE IT AND SEE IF IT NEEDS SALT. JOB DONE. OBVIOUSLY GREAT ON PASTA OR ANYTHING WITH TOMATOES – BUT ALSO VERY NICE ON A WEE NEW AYRSHIRE TATTIE, BOILED.

CHAPTER 4: BLOOD CALLS TO BLOOD

Around the time I hit 21, there were three big things in my life. Firstly, I was reconciling myself to doing a typing course while I waited for something better to come along. Second, I was toiling to sustain a moderately enjoyable medium-distance relationship with my boyfriend Ralph, despite lack of phones, transport, or parental approval on his side of the equation. And third was my mother's cancer.

I'd bought a moped on the strength of a summer job at Mauchline Creamery, and it gave me more joy than anything else I'd ever possessed. She was a red Honda Novio 50CC with a top speed of 33mph, if you were going downhill and had the wind behind you. I loved her. She was my first personal transport and, having grown up in a no-car family, she represented liberation. I could go where and when I wanted, albeit slowly and with limited comfort. I didn't care. I'd managed to drive up to Ralph's in Glasgow once or twice, using an old tramp's trick that someone told me about – you spread a newspaper up your jumper and it keeps the cold out. As I stripped off in her front sitting room, I could see the speech bubbles forming above

Ralph's mother's head: 'What on earth does he see in her?'; closely followed by, 'Where did I go wrong?'

A kind and busy District Nurse used to visit my mother that summer, before the final hospitalisation. Her husband was some kind of manager at the Creamery, and she used to pick him up at clocking-out time. I hung back one day after my cheese-packing shift, and accosted her; nobody would tell me anything about my mother's condition and I didn't know how to find out. Asking my mother directly was beyond me. The nurse told me to follow their car home on my bike, took me into her kitchen, gave me a cup of tea and helped me understand that my mother wasn't going to get any better. In fact, she would die in due course, at a time she couldn't predict but she thought it might be quite soon. Within a year, for example. I never cried in front of people; but I was crying. After a while she offered to drive me home but I insisted I could drive safely, and off I went, wobbling. I needed to come to terms with my mother's condition without letting her know I knew. We weren't able, either of us, to have that conversation.

Should I give up my place on the postgrad secretarial course at Strathclyde University to deal with all this? No, no, urged the nurse. I was tempted, though. Daunted by what was ahead of me. Doing anything different, however, would take too much energy to plan, and I had to do something to bring in some money; so I stuck with the typing course. And as it happened, my mother was admitted to hospital just as the course started, so I didn't actually have to worry about her being alone in the house all day.

Braving the elements to drive to the south side of Glasgow once in a while to see your boyfriend was one thing; but I knew I couldn't drive the moped up to Glasgow on the colder, shortening days of the winter term. Getting student digs in Glasgow was out of the question; I had to stay at home for hospital visiting. The buses to Glasgow were too infrequent, and expensive. But another option materialised. My friend Linda from school days was doing a degree at Glasgow, but living with her boyfriend – how risqué for our times! – in a caravan at Catrine House, en route for Mauchline and Glasgow. It was agreed I'd drive the moped over to hers and then she'd give me a lift, and bring me back at night. We'd share the petrol money.

Leaving home at 7am in the Scottish winter was a bitter, determined job; but arriving through mud and dead leaves at Linda's was a different matter. The caravan was all warm and cosy and sleepy, the flavour of love and languor hanging in the air. A guitar propped against the bunk, a gas burner raising a little steam, the smell of toast. Then off we'd clatter in her Fiat 500. It restored my sense that life might still be full of promise.

The secretarial course was not at all what I had imagined for myself; but I'd found myself short of options. We had to learn shorthand (Teeline) and typing (manual machines, alternating with the new-fangled electric golfball typewriters) plus office practice, and how to take orders from your boss even if you didn't agree with his way of doing things (it would invariably be a he, not a she). Optional modules included languages and various kinds of business studies. I chose French and Marketing; but had to give up Marketing because in the first class, the lecturer used a cancer analogy to describe some aspect of British industrial or commercial life. It might have been the Unions; I can't remember. It was his expression, '… like a cancer' that rocked me. I had to steer myself on a narrow little line of denial during the daytime, not touching the sides of my tunnel, so as to get through to the evening routine. I couldn't have my two lives intruding on each other. When I was training my fingers to type I wasn't fretting about my mother.

So I asked for a change of Option, and enrolled on Beginners'

Business Italian instead. I was already doing French, having studied it for two years at University. 'Be a bilingual secretary,' people said to me, and I thought it would be a standby in case I never made it into anything more interesting. Business language in both French and Italian was very flowery. So, before I properly knew how to conjugate a verb in Italian, I was learning phrases and writing letters like, 'Dear Sir, we acknowledge with humble gratitude your receipt for our Bill of Lading dated 14th inst, and assure you of our most respectful service at all times ...' and stuff like that. Bill of Lading? Don't ask me. What I do remember of Italian vocabulary back then is *'fritto misto'*, which had such a nourishing, reassuring sound. I looked it up – rabbit, chicken, liver, bacon, maybe cooked al fresco over aromatic twigs. Ah, that would be something!

Night-times after getting home were cold and rushed. I'd have cheese or egg or beans on toast and then get back out onto the bike. We had a coal fire but as the house had been empty all day while I was at Uni, and going out again soon, it wasn't worth the bother of lighting it, so I used a little electric convection heater to blow away the cold air.

Visiting Mum in hospital required a lot of self-management for us both; and we would have our conversations about how she was feeling, and how my studies were going, and whether I'd remembered to pay the rent, and to give her regards to Ralph when I saw him, and whether there had been any letters. She got letters from Mae and Roddy in London; I got letters from Ralph, and also from Marian, who had gone to France as an au pair. Her letters were fat bundles of six or seven pages of adventures, stuffed into red-and-blue-barred envelopes with foreign stamps, a great distraction for Mum and me, helping us both to avoid other current events like chemotherapy, radiotherapy, hair loss, bone marrow secondaries, blood transfusions. After I got back home at night, once a week I'd go up to the phone box with a pile of ten pences and phone Mae or Roddy to let them know how things were. It was a chilling, exhausting time.

One morning, driving up to Glasgow with Linda, I asked her for ideas about what I could eat at nights that would be quick and tasty and cheap. 'Liver,' she said. Liver? I'd never eaten liver since primary school dinners, and the memory wasn't edifying. 'Oh no,' said Linda, 'liver's great,' and she went on to describe it in words I can't remember; but her enthusiasm was convincing. That night after classes, walking back along Argyle Street to meet her, I went into Littlewoods and had a look at their butcher counter. Ox liver was only 25p a pound. It looked dark and glossy and at that price I was certainly willing to give it a try. So I bought a quarter and stuck it in my bag along with my shorthand notebook and 'Italian For Secretaries', and continued on my way.

Linda's advice was to dress it in a bit of salt-and-peppered flour, then fry it quickly on both sides – having first fried a sliced onion nice and crispy. I was starving – I was always starving although I'd never gone properly hungry all my life – and followed her instructions to the letter. The sweet pungency of frying onions set the shadows shrinking; and that dark, slippery liver – it was calling out to me, by name. Flesh to flesh. Announcing Hope. Leading me on to a better life. Onto the plate with a big mound of onions – slicing through like butter at the touch of my knife. The cowshed scent! Its bloodiness! Around my mouth and down my throat! I can still feel its animal spirit permeating me, life beckoning to life, reaching all my cold corners, gratifying and comforting and steeling me up. I was having a spiritual experience right there in my mother's kitchen as I mopped up the greasy juices with a bit of plain loaf outsidey.

Later on in the ward, I regaled my mother with the story of my cooking adventure. She approved heartily and referred me back to her NAAFI cookbook. Despite the havoc being wrought in her

blood and bone marrow, she had a strong grip on life herself –
still with a decent head of hair despite her radiotherapy and
chemo. Smudging lipstick on her cheeks for visiting time. 'You
need to look after yourself,' was her final comment on the liver
story, and we both knew what she meant.

NOSE TO TAIL EATING

As a nation, we have become ridiculously fussy about what we will eat; and nowadays, eating liver is almost unknown to most people. Being brought up poor, I learned by choice and necessity how to make the best out of the cheapest ingredients. This means every bit of the animal, not just the tender lean bits. However it's not just about managing within your budget – it's also about feeding the world. Fergus Henderson coined the term 'Nose to Tail Eating' in his 2004 cookbook of the same name; and Hugh Fearnley Whittingstall expands on the theme in his book, 'Meat'. In a world where many people go hungry; and where the burgeoning middle classes of formerly-poor nations are adopting Western habits of high-volume meat-eating – we all need to eat less meat. And if we're going to eat meat at all, we need to make sure it's reared to high welfare standards, and make good use of the whole animal, not just take the 'best' bits and chuck the rest out. (Or I suppose you could go completely vegetarian; or even vegan. But that's not for me.)

That's the worthy bit. In terms of flavour, however, it also makes great sense. You can fry up a lovely slice of liver more

QUICKLY THAN YOU CAN HEAT A READY MEAL IN THE MICROWAVE. AND IT'S SO NUTRITIOUS, FULL OF IRON AND VITAMINS. I'M NOT GOING TO ADD TO LINDA'S INSTRUCTIONS, GIVEN TO ME MORE THAN 40 YEARS AGO – THEY'RE ALREADY PERFECT, AND YOU CAN FOLLOW THEM IN MY TEXT, OR LOOK IT UP ON THE INTERNET. BUT I DO URGE YOU TO GIVE IT A GO. PLENTY WELL-FRIED ONIONS AND A GOOD DOLLOP OF BUTTERY MASH, WITH SOME NICE FRESH GREENS AND THE PAN JUICES POURED OVER. YUM YUM. IF YOU'RE GOING THROUGH HARD TIMES, THIS IS THE RECIPE THAT WILL GIVE YOU COURAGE AND ENDURANCE. SO, IN MY MOTHER'S WORDS – LOOK AFTER YOURSELF.

CHAPTER 5: HORSEMEAT AND OYSTERS

Marian ended up spending ten years in France – our entire 20s – and I had the brilliant opportunity of visiting her on a regular basis, meeting her friends, joining in her French life, and learning a bit about things I'd hitherto only known in textbooks. It was shaming to discover that, despite my seven years' enthusiastic study of the French language, I could barely keep up a conversation with Marian's boss's six-year-old granddaughter. So I had the chance to improve on my French as well as joining in with the local ways.

After my mother's passing I had moved to Glasgow, and continued to cook for friends. On one occasion I commandeered the whole of a (small) shared flat to conjure up a meal for four, and vividly remember the mammoth clear-up operation afterwards. There really wasn't the space, or the equipment, to do anything very fancy; but I didn't perceive that as a barrier. Hence the mess. 'Entertaining' back then was quite formal and maybe even aspirational – so it was three rich courses with wine; then coffee – with liqueurs, no less. I cooked a chicken and peanut dish from a Marks and Spencer cookbook, and remember (a) being quite stressed in its preparation, and (b) that it turned out to be absolutely delicious. I loved it, and so did my guests, and I bathed for a while in the accolade. On another occasion I served up a chilli con carne so vast in its proportions, all plated, that my five-foot-nothing shrimp of a guest fainted dead away. No, I'm exaggerating of course – she merely lost her appetite. Not a great result either. I needed to learn about portion sizes; but my flavours were good.

Marian's letters from France, meantime, were full of intriguing comments on the food scene over there. She mentioned *andouillette*, a sausage made with intestines and tripe; and how she had been terribly sick as a result of eating one. She talked about salad dressing, and she wasn't referring to Heinz Salad Cream. She got a job on a farm where they bred goats, ducks and rabbits, and produced goats' cheeses, and duck and rabbit terrines. When she came home on holiday and I visited her at Langholm, her mum allowed her to cook for 'the birthday girls' – herself and six friends – and was stressed out by Marian's apparently careless approach. Marian and I had gone off to Ayr for a *sortie* on the afternoon of the event and Mrs Mitchell had peeled a ton of potatoes because she knew we wouldn't have time. 'Potatoes?' said Marian, not a bit grateful. 'We're not having *potatoes*.' So there was this mother–daughter dynamic, whereby Marian declined to learn from her brilliant cook of a mother, while I learned loads. She and Mrs Mitchell had a bit of a rebellion thing going on, and meantime in her formative cooking years, Marian learned an entirely different way of doing things – a French way, quite different from what was going on in Scotland; simple yet elegant.

I meantime kept well in touch with Mrs Mitchell from my new home in Glasgow, and continued to be influenced by her gracious way of doing things. She was a keen learner too, and wanted to know what I was cooking – I was humbled. At the same time, I had the rare opportunity to learn something about

French cooking, and eating, both first- and second-hand from Marian.

On her farm on the Picardie/Normandie border, she was put in charge of making four types of terrine: rabbit *ordinaire*; rabbit *mariné*, duck *ordinaire*, and duck *au poivre vert* – with green peppercorns. This was all done in an outhouse with a wood-fired oven. She skinned the rabbits; plucked the ducks; and minced the meats, with fatty pork, into a baby's bath which served as a giant mixing bowl. Then it was all pounded by hand and pressed into oval terracotta terrine dishes with lids, and baked in the oven. This was a job requiring strength. I'd have been useless at it.

She also milked the goats (only two teats as I discovered), and the farmer made the cheeses. Some of these were kept for maturing, and others sold fresh – so there were three types of goat cheese to sell – *frais, demi-sec,* and *sec.* The sec ones were less than a quarter the size of the frais, and extremely pungent. Gorgeous, actually; farmyardy.

In pear season, they made pear cakes in a sort of clafoutis style, dropping juicy long slices of freshly-peeled pear into batter in foil flan cases.

Four or five days of the week, Marian loaded up the van and took the farm's wares to local markets. 'Local' might mean up to 45 minutes' drive away, so these were early starts. If I was visiting her on market days I went along and 'helped'. I remember cold black mornings and having to leave her flat without breakfast, which was a first for me, and a bit of a shocker. Competing for prime corner spots on the marketplace was part of the deal; on one occasion we set off the night before for a particularly important market – a *foire*, a big kind of festival event. Marian managed to slide the van into a corner spot normally taken by a bunch of men from some other stall, and we hid in the back of the van till after dark while they battered the sides of the van with their fists, mad that their place had been taken and determined to make us move on. But we held our ground. I was amazed at Marian's bravery, or effrontery. Imagine doing all that on your own!

After getting the stall set up in the morning there would be coffee and croissants from a nearby *boulangerie*; and the customers started early. We had a little set of brass scales with weights in grammes, and people asked for specific quantities by the gramme, which seemed very 'other' to me – everything at home was solidly imperial back then. This was good number-language practice – *deux-cents cinquante grammes* at so many francs and centimes per kilo, and endless variations – all at customers' normal talking pace. Marian eased away their irritation at my slowness by explaining that I was her friend from Scotland, and they said 'Scotland? You are from Scotland Marian? We didn't know that.' And they welcomed me, and complimented me on my French (eeek) and it was all very cheery. Then they would take away their little parcels of terrine, to serve as a course on its own or a little lunch, and their pungent or fresh little cheeses. I wondered at the expense, and how people afforded it, and it turned out that our stall was of the gourmet variety, ready to assist the local bourgeoisie in disposing of their surplus cash and entertaining their guests *comme il faut*. How intriguing; another delightful experience for me.

There was a *chevaline*, or horsemeat stall, on one of the markets and the *patron* and Marian had struck up some acquaintance. She asked if I would like to taste horsemeat and of course I said yes. So one day she left me with her stall while she went and placed our order, which we would collect at the end of trading. But we forgot – so, later that afternoon, we headed off to Monsieur le Chevaline's home where he welcomed us in and gave us a glass of wine and introduced us to his wife and children. On the living-room wall was mounted a long silky black horse's tail, at real horse's-bottom height, which made it look as if the horse was in the next room, poking its tail through a hole in the wall. Back at Marian's we ate the steaks which were as tender as could be, and well-flavoured. It seems that horsemeat, like every other kind of meat, has its various cuts; and ours was best fillet. My experience of best fillet anything, including beef, has always been patchy and occasional, so I wouldn't be the best person to explain the difference between horse and cow in terms of flavour or texture. However I do remember thinking that if I hadn't known it was horsemeat – seen its very tail on the wall, no less – I wouldn't have guessed. Maybe that would be an insult to a horsemeat vendor; maybe they strive for differentiation. In any case, I loved it.

I spent an Easter with Marian one year, when she was living with a friend and his father in a little village in Picardie. Her friend's father conversed cordially with me but said in an aside to Marian, 'elle a la mauvaise mine,' which translated as 'she's far too pale.' His recommendation to address this shortcoming was that I should be drinking considerably more red wine, and soon I would have a ruddy complexion to match his own.

There was a stately home of some kind in the village – Monsieur worked for the owner at times, and we were invited to tour the gardens after lunch. Marian had invited half a dozen friends to join us, and had remembered me expressing an interest in oysters. I'd probably read about them in some novel or other, and been charmed by their romance. As usual, Marian was working at the market that morning, and brought twelve of the gnarly grey molluscs home with her in a paper bag. She produced a sharp, stabbing sort of little knife with a short blade and proceeded to open them up, waving away my offer of help. I realised this was a skilled operation, and these were expensive wee beasties, and she knew how clumsy I could be – enough said.

I was taken aback by the contents of the shells. Very gloopy. But even more taken aback when she explained what she was doing with her little knife – cutting the oyster's connecting tissue to the shell – effectively, killing it just before it was eaten. This was the closest I'd ever come to the slaughter of innocent beasts in pursuit of human greed (I'd obviously forgotten about the turkeys and hens), and I was a bit shocked. But my good manners, thanks to my mother's school of hard knocks, were unfailing; and I was grateful for Marian's generous hospitality, especially since she herself was allergic to the wee beasts and couldn't eat them.

Fortunately by this time second gins had been poured, and like a pro, I raised a shell to my lips at the appointed hour, and slurped. Chewed. Swallowed. Marian had prepared a little vinaigrette to dress the dismembered little jellies, and the combination of gin, tonic, oil and lemon juice with the cool slitherers was surprisingly agreeable. Maybe by this time there was also champagne on the go; that would have been typical, and could only have enhanced my rapidly increasing appreciation. My mother would have been proud of me; her sago lessons a success. I managed my full share – along with the rest of the meal, which involved roasted pork served with Monsieur's stored flageolet beans from the previous year's harvest. Later, with our friends (her friends really, but we were all full of *entente cordiale* by that time), we were conducted round the grounds of the stately home and I remember having to concentrate very carefully so as not to collapse into a drunken heap behind the *parterre*. It was a very good Easter.

FAUX FILET, ANYONE?

In 2013, across Europe, a scandal broke in which a number of ready meals labelled as containing beef were found to contain horsemeat. There was a major outcry. But interestingly in the long run, it did the French horsemeat trade no real harm. The true culprit was recognised – it was the ready meal industry, where people had lost connection with the food they were eating and didn't know how to tell the difference between good and bad, or one meat and another. So the issue was about traceability and labelling rather than the eating of horses.

Eating horsemeat in France was traditionally a working-class preference, as it was cheaper than beef. Although horsemeat consumption has dropped, there has been a resurgence of interest in recent years from a younger clientele – partly because horsemeat is low in both fat and cholesterol. I wonder if there are parallels with venison in the UK. I remember having a conversation with a young Italian student about what kind of Scottish food was good to eat, and I was trying to explain venison. She couldn't figure it out from my

DESCRIPTIONS AND EVENTUALLY I REMEMBERED THE CHILDREN'S FILM, 'BAMBI'. 'AH, BAMBI!' SHE CRIED, INSTANTLY TUNED IN. 'DELICIOUS!' – AND ON THE FOLLOWING MONDAY MORNING SHE LEANED ACROSS HER LAPTOP IN THE LIBRARY AND WHISPERED, 'I ATE BAMBI YESTERDAY!'

CHAPTER 6: BREAST MILK AND BOURGETTES

Around age 30 I became mega-broody and I truly couldn't believe I would find happiness without a baby or so in my life – as unexpected a turn of events for my husband, Bernard, as it was for me. However conception took longer than expected, and then when I did conceive, I wasn't very good at hanging onto the precious little bundles. I was obsessed; if we were walking along the street and a pregnant woman hove into view in the far distance, Bernard would shove me up a close before I saw her because – the moods, the moods! Anyway, we were blessed in due course with a fabulous baby boy whom we called Harry. (Not sure if this was a subliminal connection, but the night before I was to go into hospital to be induced, we went with Roddy to the cinema to see 'When Harry Met Sally'. Meg Ryan's fake orgasm in the deli was inspiring; but nothing like as dramatic as my heaving on the couch the next day.)

I was determined to breastfeed, but we were going through an era when it wasn't particularly promoted in Scotland. I'd found a National Childbirth Trust antenatal group nearby and attended enthusiastically. The breastfeeding adviser gave us lots of practical info and it was just as well, because there was nothing in the hospital to encourage you. Back then, you spent five whole days in hospital for a 'normal' birth (ten for a caesarean), so that they could check you out and make sure you weren't going to do terrible things to your little sprogling. Right at the start I managed brilliantly. The midwives, two sturdy angels, had gone off to recover from my heaving, leaving me with a cup of tea and a baby lying in the cot by my side.

He was beautiful. I'd been warned not to expect an oil painting because apparently some babies look terrible immediately after they've been born. But not mine; I couldn't keep my eyes off him. As he lay there, he started pursing his lips in a sucking motion, which I interpreted as hunger. The midwives had said that when they came back from their tea and toast, they'd clean me up and help me with the first feed – but they showed no sign of returning. Not being in any way experienced with babies I wanted to do as the experts bade me; but I couldn't watch my baby go hungry. I thought I'd better have a go on my own; and since my entire body felt like a bag of loose parts, I thought it was more than likely the midwives would return anyway before I managed to manoeuvre myself into a seated position.

I was still lying in the bloody sheets; but I managed to hitch myself up a bit and swivel round to get my feet on the floor. Still no sign of the midwives so biting my lip, I reached into the crib and figured out a way of lifting the wee bundle without letting his head dangle. The lipsmacking grew faster and louder. The NCT adviser had said that it wasn't just a case of getting your nipple in, it was the whole mouthful of breast that encircled the nipple – what was needed was a good seal between baby's lips and mother's boob, to form a vacuum, which would make the milk shower forth. Or something along those lines. Anyway, still no sign of the midwives so I followed NCT advice, hoping I wasn't smothering him – and lo and behold, on he latched and was sucking for Scotland! It was the most wonderful feeling. After a while I remembered that you're supposed to change them round so that both breasts get emptied evenly, and I managed that too, after a fashion. He slowed down a bit and we were sitting together in rapt, dozy harmony when the midwives came back to the labour suite, antennae raised because I wasn't lying supine as they'd left me. 'Oh!' said one of them, 'you're feeding him ...' and she consulted my notes hanging on the end of the bed. 'I thought this was your first baby?' They virtually had to widen the doorway to get me back to the ward, such was the size of my head at this accolade. 'I was right!' I told myself. 'This is what I was born for!'

As the euphoria wore off, so did the milk flow. The following night I was sitting up at 3am ('Every four hours! Nothing in between!') trying to get Harry to feed, but he wouldn't pay attention. The senior midwife on duty came in and waved her finger at him: 'Young man, if you don't learn to do this properly, your mother will have breasts like turnips!' He still didn't pay attention but at least I got a laugh. 'Turnips' in Scotland aren't those sweet white little globes, but muckle lumpy great purple swedes, a perfect description of my poor boobs at that time.

When I was discharged I was given an info sheet which included a strong recommendation for breastfeeding mothers – we were to drink a can of Tennent's Sweetheart Stout each day – it was supposed to help your milk supply. So I take back all that I said about not much support for breastfeeding, because this was the greatest support you could possibly wish for, in the sleep-deprived state of shock that all new mothers experience. It was 2% ABV, sweet and dark and malty, and to be able to kick back in a reclining armchair with your precious baby under one arm, sooking peacefully – and yourself sooking from the can with the aid of the other arm – the telly on with 'Take the High Road' or some other Scottish soap trundling on through its dramatic highs and lows – this made motherhood seem just about feasible. Breast milk flowed much more freely this way, with the pressure to perform for the nurses switched off, and the four-hour rule abandoned.

Weaning was to start at 20 weeks, not a day sooner. It involved baby rice in tiny quantities, from a spoon, with breast milk still the main event; and gradually increasing the amount and range of 'solids'. I really enjoyed this phase – partly because of the joy and responsibility of introducing a new little being to a good healthy diet, and partly also, I must be honest, in anticipation of getting my boobs back. No more tucking a baby under your jumper in public places and glaring at anyone who dared raise an eyebrow.

A fresh pear, peeled, diced and briefly microwaved, quickly turns to mush and was seized on with joy by Harry. A mashed avocado – less so. Everything mashable got mashed and soon enough we had a good repertoire going. It was very satisfying, watching him thrive and grow, nourished by the best of stuff. I didn't make much use of jars, although they were handy for out and about; I wanted to cook from scratch, and before too long we were all eating the same thing at teatime, with his a little more mashed and mixed than ours.

I still liked cooking liver occasionally (Nutritious! Tasty! Cheap!) and tried it on the three-year-old Harry one day. He was quite curious about its appearance, and took his spoon to it quite readily. However his face changed as soon as the mush hit his mouth, with rank disgust writ large; 'Me no like eatin jobbies!' he uttered, much to his father's merriment (sometimes I have to recognise that not everyone has such a sophisticated palate as me). 'Oh, son,' says Bernard, slapping his thigh, 'I'd never get away with saying that!'

On the whole, Harry ate whatever we gave him, which was usually healthy and fresh. Some veggies, however, weren't going down too well. His older cousin Simon used to come and spend some of his days with us when his mother was working, and at teatime I thought I'd have a second go at introducing spinach. 'I don't like spinach,' came the immediate response from Harry, now aged about five, as I put the plates down in front of them. I looked at Simon, who was quietly getting stuck in.

'It's not spinach,' I said, 'it's minach.' Two small faces looking puzzled. I winked at Simon while Harry repeated, 'minach? I've never seen minach before.'

Simon, two and a half years older than Harry, found our little conspiracy hilarious. He was fed up with a cousin who never wanted to play football with him but always had his nose stuck in a book. He aided and abetted me with élan, and by the end of the meal Harry had cleared his plate and was saying quite contentedly, 'minach is okay.'

A week later I worked the same trick. 'These aren't courgettes, these are bourgettes.'

'Yum,' said Simon, 'I love bourgettes.'

'Me too,' I said, 'and they're very good for you.'

'Do they make you good at reading?' asked Simon.

'Yeah.' Another set of clean plates. This time, Simon and I couldn't conceal our glee and Harry had to be brought in on the joke. He was indignant. Simon and I were rolling around holding our sides with mirth. Ice cream was deployed in making the peace but what a laugh! It was worth it. After all, it's a mother's duty to teach her children to enjoy a healthy diet. Isn't it?

We made flapjacks; we made Chelsea buns. The buns were Simon's idea and pretty complicated for an eight and a five year old; actually, pretty complicated for a 38 year old, but I've never allowed complications in recipes to put me off. They actually turned out brilliantly, and Simon in particular was entranced. What really appealed to him was the construction bit, where you spread your dough with mincemeat and roll it up into a sausage, then slice the sausage and arrange the slices, cut side up, in a circle in a tin for baking. And then of course the flavour, which was magnificent. In later life Simon became a chef, and I take a tiny little bit of credit for his early fascination with cooking.

We had a holiday in Denmark when Simon came too, and Harry learned to ask for a strawberry ice cream in Danish. After we returned home, I had an Italian colleague stay overnight, and we were telling Laura about our holiday. She taught Harry to pronounce '*gelato di fragola*'. A child can't have too many translations in his repertoire for strawberry ice cream, can he? You never know when it will come in handy. After his bedtime, Laura and I were sitting out in the garden with a glass of wine, when a little parachute came fluttering down from Harry's bedroom above. There was a little note in its basket: 'please can I have some gelato di fragola?' That's my boy.

STRAWBERRY FIELDS FOREVER

IF YOU DRIVE ALONG THE NORTH BANK OF THE RIVER TAY, KNOWN AS THE CARSE OF GOWRIE, YOU WILL SEE POLYTUNNELS STRETCHING FOR MILES AND MILES. THEY'RE NOT AS SCENIC AS THE UNCOVERED RASPBERRY AND STRAWBERRY FIELDS USED TO BE, BUT THEY'RE A LOT MORE PRODUCTIVE AND HAVE EXTENDED THE SCOTTISH SOFT FRUIT SEASON HUGELY. THIS IS GOOD NEWS FOR ANYONE WHO LOVES A SWEET FRESH BERRY; BUT ALSO FOR LEGIONS OF PICKERS AND PACKERS, MANY OF WHOM CAME FROM EASTERN EUROPE MANY SEASONS AGO, AND STAYED TO BRING UP FAMILIES HERE. FOR THE LAST FEW YEARS, THE UK'S PROTRACTED BREXIT PROCESS HAS MADE LIFE PRETTY UNCERTAIN FOR MANY OF THEM AND WE'RE ALL CROSSING OUR FINGERS THAT THE MADNESS WILL SOON SETTLE DOWN AND WE CAN ALL GET ON WITH OUR LIVES.

MEANTIME, STRAWBERRY AND RASPBERRY JAMS ARE A GREAT FAVOURITE HERE, WITH JAM FRUIT COSTING MUCH LESS AT WAYSIDE STALLS THAN THE BIGGER, MORE PERFECT BERRIES. THEY REALLY MAKE THE TASTE OF SUMMER LAST, AND ARE A GOOD THING TO HAVE IN THE CUPBOARD, OR TAKE AS A GIFT. HOWEVER, THEY ARE HIGH IN SUGAR – TYPICALLY, THE SAME AMOUNT OF SUGAR AS FRUIT IN ANY BATCH OF JAM. YOU CAN CUT IT DOWN TO HALF THE QUANTITY OF SUGAR TO

FRUIT, USING JAM SUGAR OR SOME LEMON JUICE IN THE CASE OF STRAWBERRIES TO MAKE SURE IT SETS. THEN AFTER BREAKING THE SEAL IN THE JAR, KEEP IT IN THE FRIDGE FOR UP TO A MONTH.

OR YOU COULD BUY YOUR JAM FROM ANOTHER KEEN JAM MAKER, AND USE YOUR OWN BERRIES TO MAKE A GORGEOUS SUMMERY COCKTAIL WHICH IS FOREVER IN MY MIND EMBLEMATIC OF MY FRIENDS DONNA AND RHONA. DONNA IS FROM ARKANSAS, AND AFTER WORK ONE DAY TAUGHT RHONA AND ME TO DRINK STRAWBERRY DAIQUIRIS (AND ON ANOTHER OCCASION, MARGARITAS – BUT THAT'S ANOTHER STORY).

BEST TO MEASURE THE SPIRITS – JUST TO RETAIN SOME SENSE OF CONTROL.

CRUSH A PILE OF ICE CUBES USING YOUR FAVOURITE METHOD (POLY BAG AND ROLLING PIN SUITS ME) AND PUT THEM IN A BLENDER GOBLET. ADD 100ML WHITE RUM, MAYBE HALF A POUND OF STRAWBERRIES, A COUPLE OF TABLESPOONS OF LIME JUICE, FRESHLY SQUEEZED IF YOU CAN GET HOLD OF THEM, AND GIVE IT A WHIZZ. TASTE AND ADD A BIT OF ICING SUGAR, IF NEEDED, TO SWEETEN A LITTLE. POUR INTO 3 OR 4 GLASSES AND TOAST YOUR FRIENDS. REPEAT.

CHAPTER 7: CHRISTMAS DINNERS

Cookbooks are such a source of delight. Elegance, inspiration, happy well-fed faces all around the table. Likewise, cookery magazines, of which I must have devoured a few million in my lifetime. However as the years go by you do notice a certain predictability with the seasonal numbers, and never moreso than at Christmas.

Delia Smith was the empress of my generation of home cooks. There had been plenty other television cookery programmes before hers, but they mainly featured male chefs, and a certain formality, or a showy style of doing things. Delia directed her attentions towards people cooking at home, and she unashamedly covered the basics (how to boil an egg) while going on to demonstrate all the lovely ways you could do things with your developing knowledge and skills. She believed in cooking from scratch, and I followed her devotedly. Which also reads as, I became a bit of a nerd in terms of not taking short cuts. Unlike other areas of my life where I was quite content to compromise on standards, I became a bit of a perfectionist – or maybe even pedant – in the kitchen. Gravy, for instance, was only gravy if you used the roasty meaty residues from yesterday's project, deglazed your pan with a little wine, enhanced with the cooking water from your broccoli and so on. I adopted completely Delia's abhorrence of stock cubes. And that's only the start of it. No harm done, in fact a positive advantage in many ways; except that it could be tricky to fit it all in along with the day job, the rest of life, and the toddler/growing child, husband and house to see to. It didn't matter, I limped along and enjoyed what I cooked, and so did other people.

Christmas was a different matter, however. The wide-ranging ideas in the cookery magazines always coalesced into what they called 'the big event' – the turkey. And Delia was as precise as ever in her recommendations. She evoked such a sense of domestic order, comfort and joy, peace to all mankind in her Christmas writing – listening to King's College Choir on Christmas Eve while she mixed her three kinds of stuffing – it was hard to resist. Also waving to me from the turkey camp was my mother and the nine-year-old me, capering around at Barturk Farm where she went after school dinner duties in November and December every year, hoisting, drawing necks, and plucking her way through dozens of the proud gobblers. She and two other strong women, a harmonious and efficient Christmas Dinner Machine, standing there in the barn with a rapidly balding turkey lurching and squawking in its death throes as the feathers flew.

So, thirty years later, I found it hard to throw off the turkey requirement, along with its very precise accompaniments à la Delia. Not only the perfectly roasted bird but also the range of stuffings, the cranberry sauce, the bread sauce, the chipolatas, three or four hot fresh veggies including sprouts with chestnuts, perfectly roasted potatoes as well as a little mound of buttery mash, and the gravy. All fresh and hot on the table at the same time. It was a trial. One was obliged to buy a massive bird because of the joy (?) of dealing with all the leftovers. And a big turkey is a challenge to cook well. Every year I basted and roasted and turned it over, employing all the tricks in my battery. I suppose it usually turned out well enough, but by the time it hit the table, I was sick of it. One year, working full time, I was late in acquiring my turkey and fretfully settled for a frozen one. We left it in the utility room to defrost, and early on Christmas morning I found our cat Jet halfway up its arse, headfirst. Sorry for the language, it comes to me very readily when I think about cooking turkeys. Not another f***ing turkey, I would think drearily, as Christmas came round again.

We always had Bernard's mum, Lily, with us on Christmas Day. She was a cheerful, sociable, appreciative wee woman most of the time but somehow, on that particular day of the year, she often had a fit of the blues. Probably remembering her family life back home in Glasgow when she was the youngest of a huge family, and told it like it was Walton's Mountain. Or missing her two dead husbands.

I needed a drink to get Christmas dinner on the table. Just a couple of gin and tonics, and then the sharing of a bottle of wine with the meal. But Lily was horrified at the prospect of getting a taxi home after the meal because once, many years ago, a pensioner in the papers had been raped by a taxi driver on Christmas Day. She wouldn't countenance spending the night with us; so Bernard had to stay sober till after he'd driven her home. Leaving me as the only one drinking. Can you feel my pain?

I decided to change things. No more f***ing turkeys in our house. Sorry Mum. No-one round our table really cared what they ate, but they probably cared that I ended up tipsy, stressed and crabbit. I still wanted to do a lovely meal. One year I tried cooking a salmon in the dishwasher, as demonstrated by some other TV cook (but probably not Delia). I should have practiced beforehand. It worked out fine, but only after two cycles of the dishwasher because they didn't tell you on the telly to get a

SMALL salmon, and mine was huge. And I should have done it in advance instead of doing it the F.T. way, aiming for all the other parts of the meal to be ready at the same time. So it was an extended period at table that year, but with a few laughs at my expense, and Lily was intrigued out of her blues at such a crazy idea as cooking a salmon in a dishwasher.

The following year I went a bit further, and decided to do a Christmas dinner from another country's repertoire. After mulling it around for a while I decided Caribbean would be good – cheery and a bit different. I visited Clarissa Dickson Wright's Books for Cooks at the bottom of Victoria Street in Edinburgh, and had a lovely browse around. Eventually I chose 'Trade Winds: A Caribbean Cookery Book', which helped me produce the menu for Christmas 2002:

- *Chilled Avocado Soup, served with Garlic Bread*
- *Trinidad Fried Prawns*
- *Boucan Pork*
- *Sauteed Sweet Potatoes, Spinach, Okra, Rice and Peas*
- *Coconut ice cream with lime sauce*

(For the soup, blend a couple of avocados with chicken stock, milk, a small green pepper, spring onions, a little olive oil, 2 tsp coriander seeds, crushed; a dash of Tabasco and a tablespoon of tomato ketchup. Season to taste with salt and pepper. The Boucan Pork recipe involved soft brown sugar, dark rum, garlic, fresh root ginger, cloves and coriander seed. It was great. The dessert was a retreat to Delia Smith but went beautifully.)

Bob Marley crooned along in the background and the gin was swapped for rum. I was a little apprehensive about Lily's response to chilled soup; but I needn't have been. She enjoyed new experiences and was hugely diverted by such a novel Christmas lunch, with which she'd be able to regale her daughter the next day. Bernard and Harry enjoyed it too – it was fresh and, by normal Christmas dinner standards, light. The flavours were sour and sweet and sharp and mellow. And they probably enjoyed the improvement in my state of anxiety. All in all, it was a great success, and it has freed me for evermore from the oppression of F.T. dinners. Or any other domestic prescription that has you exhausted on your knees in a dubious quest for perfection. After all, this is a recipe for life (and not just for Christmas).

FROZEN IS THE NEW FRESH

(OR SO I'VE HEARD.)

I'M VERY FOND OF AVOCADOS. BUT THEY'RE A BIT UNPREDICTABLE WHEN YOU BUY THEM IN THE SHOPS. MAYBE NOT SO MUCH IF YOU LIVE IN THE SAME COUNTRY THEY GROW IN, BUT IN SCOTLAND, IT'S TRICKY TO BUY THEM AT THE RIGHT STAGE OF RIPENESS. PROBABLY IT'S THE FOOD MILES THAT DO IT — THEY MUST BE PICKED LONG BEFORE THEY'RE RIPE, SO THAT THEY SURVIVE THE JOURNEY. FOR NORMAL LIFE I JUST BUY THE AVOCADOS AND WAIT FOR THEM TO RIPEN AT HOME, THEN USE THEM. BUT I HAVE TENDED TO AVOID THEM FOR 'SPECIAL OCCASIONS' LIKE CHRISTMAS DINNER BECAUSE I COULDN'T BE SURE THEY'D BE OKAY ON THE DAY. UNDERRIPE AVOCADO IS NOT, AFTER ALL, A FESTIVE THING. I MUST HAVE BEEN EITHER BRAVE OR DESPERATE TO RISK IT AT CHRISTMAS 2002, AND OBVIOUSLY GOT LUCKY.

HOWEVER — DEEP JOY — YOU CAN NOW BUY FROZEN AVOCADOS IN THE SUPERMARKET. I WAS VERY SCEPTICAL THE FIRST TIME I SAW THEM, AND GAVE THEM THE BODY SWERVE. THEN I WAS IN LUPE PINTOS' DELI IN GREAT WESTERN ROAD IN GLASGOW, WHERE THEY SELL A RANGE OF LOVELY SPANISH/MEXICAN READY-MADE SALADY THINGS ON THEIR CARRY-OUT SANDWICH COUNTER. ABOVE EACH, THEY SPECIFY THE INGREDIENTS — AND LO AND BEHOLD, THEIR GUACAMOLE WAS MADE

WITH FROZEN AVOCADOS. SO HAVING TASTED THEIR EXCELLENT GUACAMOLE, I BOUGHT SOME FROZEN AVOCADOS ON THE WAY HOME AND THEY WERE DELICIOUS. AND THEY HELP YOU AVOID WASTE.

LOVE FOOD! HATE WASTE!

THAW THEM OUT AND STIR IN SOME FRESH CHILLI, GARLIC AND CHOPPED CORIANDER. ADD SOME CHOPPED TOMATOES AND CUCUMBER AND SPRING ONIONS IF YOU HAVE THEM. SMUSH IT ALL AROUND A BIT. THE CURRENT WORD ON MENUS FOR AVOCADOS IS 'SMASHED' NOT 'MASHED.' IF THESE THINGS MATTER TO YOU. SPREAD THEM ON A TORTILLA OR TWO. LOVELY.

OR FOR THE SOUP, JUST FOLLOW THE RECIPE IN MY STORY, SUBSTITUTING FROZEN AVOCADOS FOR FRESH. EASY PEASY.

CHAPTER 8: VEGGIES AND WHISKY

Having a child connects you strongly to other people with children. You tell yourself it's for the child's sake – especially with an only child – you have to make sure he has company and learns to share and all the rest of it. However it's also about your own needs to survive the shock and responsibility of parenting, the occasional exhaustion, the doubts and fears; and succumbing to the messy fun of it all. I can't imagine what my life would have been like if Harry hadn't come along. We got close to people in the street with whom we probably wouldn't otherwise have discovered much in common, and that was, mainly, great.

In Kingseat there were about eight families of us, with 15 kids between toddler and twelvish, and our sense of all being in it together instantly created a busy social calendar. We had a rash of 40th birthday parties for a start, which involved lots of babysitters – though one member during that time bucked the demographic and had a 30th birthday instead, with lots of stick from the rest of us oldies. There were plenty children's parties (aaaagh, not my favourite somehow, I found them very stressful). The best of those in my memory was when Kate and Graham hired the Carnegie Centre for a private swimming party with the floating armadillo. Or crocodile, or some other long knobbly inflatable. It was a hoot, having the chance as an adult to run along this wet rubbery thing and plunge shrieking into the water. The worst birthday party in my memory was one we held for Harry, where we hired a magician to come and do a magic show; and only later was told – possibly without clear evidence – that he had paedophile convictions. Maybe it was just somebody being malicious. Anyway it was a bit scary to think I'd invited all those children large and small into my living room for potential grooming or worse. Yes, there were plenty adults around; and I'm pretty sure nothing untoward happened; yet the memory still makes me twitch.

We also had Hogmanay parties, bonfire night events, summer barbecues, camping weekends, and any other excuse for a party we could think of. It was a really fun period of our lives. We took it in turns to host, but the food was always shared, so it was never a hassle. I loved this kind of large-scale cooking – you got to experiment with new recipes, without the exhaustion and military organisation it would have taken if you didn't have another seven families also cooking merrily away in the run-up to the event. It wasn't sophisticated, but it was good – things like chilli con carne or lasagne or quiches, with loads of salads and bread and dips and so on. Two of the women in the group were vegetarian, which raised my awareness somewhat; up till then I'd thought of vegetarianism as a cranky affectation only to be encountered among elite types. In fact early on during this period, someone asked me, 'is Kate vegetarian?' and my reply was 'no she can't be, she's from Motherwell ...' Apologies to all vegetarians and all Motherwell people. I was young and foolish.

So I started incorporating vegetarian recipes into my repertoire and enjoyed a good varied diet, rich with fish and meat as well as fruit and veg. I was beginning to recognise that lots of people made poor dietary choices, and it wasn't just about poverty – in our own big sociable circle there were children who were being given Nutella sandwiches on white bread to take to school for a packed lunch. I know I sound like a food fascist when I say that sort of thing – but really! I'm still intolerant of this. Parents should be helping their children to develop habits that will keep them in good health throughout their lives – not to put on weight and lose their teeth at an early age. Minach and bourgettes may have been deceitful, but they were healthy. Forgive the rant.

In our own little family we had lots of nice cooking opportunities too. We went camping to France every summer (Eurocamp or Canvas Holidays – large frame pre-constructed tents with proper fridges, stoves, beds, table and chairs – not proper camping at all, really! But airy and fun and with lots of facilities on campsites set in beautiful rural areas). There was the joy of the markets, with their piles of fish and fruit and veg; the boulangeries with the baguettes and croissants; the supermarkets with the tanks of lobsters swimming around waiting to be picked; the cheese – oh yes, the cheese! I was incapable of buying less than four types at a time. We had wonderful picnic feasts all round France, and I haven't even mentioned the wine yet.

I had a big operation when I was 45 (cue for Les Dawson mouthed whispers: *women's problems!*) with the joy of being off work for three months. At the point where I started to get my strength and energy back, Bernard took us to Edinburgh for an afternoon trip to the then-new farmers' market, on Castle Terrace. It was inspiring. There was a van which had driven down all the way from Ullapool, on the north-west coast, at the crack of dawn with the previous evening's catch of lobsters, crabs and langoustines. I bought a couple of big crabs, still crawling in the sack, and that night made Partan Bree. I was a bit post-operatively wiped out; but I remember sitting at the kitchen table with my recipe book, contentedly hammering and cracking my way into the shells, extracting all the briny brown and white flesh. I couldn't believe its wealth and splendour. To my amazement however, neither Bernard nor Harry would touch it – were they mad? This was truly gourmet stuff, despite its simplicity – probably the gourmet-est I'd ever made. But they were both grossed out by the fact that I'd killed live creatures in the making of a pot of soup.

I had powerful memories of my mum drawing the necks of turkeys so as to earn a little extra at Christmas; and I had spent quite a lot of time on farms in my childhood. So long as animals were well cared for in life, and killed with compassion, I had no problem with eating meat and fish. We were always so hard up as children that any kind of refusal of good food was out of the question; I could imagine my mother turning in her grave at the rejection of my Partan Bree. But what could I do about it? My mother did her best to make me eat her overboiled and totally disgusting cabbage – and she and I had terrible rows about it. Nowadays it would probably be seen as cruelty. But she had lived through the war and rationing, and couldn't bear to see food wasted. I could see her point. Anyway, I just had to freeze some of my beautiful soup for later – after I'd managed three portions in one sitting, of course! And put up with other people's misdirected foibles.

Actually in Harry's case it got worse. There had been a hog roast at the farmers' market – the first we'd ever seen – and this further disgusted him, to the point that he announced the next day that henceforth he was going veggie. Bloody hell. Two of the nicest culinary treats in my life, and my son was eschewing meat and fish as a result? I argued and cajoled and refused to cook two different things for tea – he could take it or leave it. However in the longer run (and his veggie period lasted for four whole years), I incorporated more veggie stuff into the general menu, and he compromised by eating a bit of fish and chicken. Not a vegetarian at all, you might say if you were being high-principled; but thank goodness I said, a growing boy needs his protein.

Around this time, I wrote a short story set in a whisky distillery, and someone suggested it would make a good first chapter for a novel. So I set about researching the whisky industry and visited lots of distilleries and a bottling plant, and had an interview with someone from the Scotch Whisky Association. The research was wonderful – writing the novel much harder. I should probably have left it as a short story; but I pressed on regardless.

One October we drove all the way north to Scrabster near John O'Groats (the airport being fogged out) and caught the ferry to Stromness, in Orkney, where we had a wild and windy holiday. Prehistoric relics surrounded us, astonishingly well-preserved through the millenia. Darkness settled early on our hired cottage, with a coy green glimmering suggestion of Northern Lights in the sky. Seals slipped and dipped quietly around the rocks. It was highly atmospheric. With a dram of Highland Park inside me and in the lee of the ancient stone circles, I completed my first ever full-length draft of a novel. The next day, we packed up and caught a pitching-and-tossing ferry back to the mainland. In due course I decided that it was a rubbish novel, but right then, clinging and lurching around on the ploughing deck, I was elated; I was a writer.

SOME GOOD THINGS TO TAKE TO A
BRING-AND-SHARE BUFFET PARTY

AUBERGINE PARMIGIANA: BRUSH THE SLICES OF AUBERGINE WITH OIL AND BAKE THEM ALL IN THE OVEN FOR 20–30 MINUTES BEFORE LAYERING THEM UP WITH A GARLICKY TOMATO SAUCE. FINISH ON TOP WITH SOME KIND OF CHEESE SAUCE AND BAKE THE WHOLE THING FOR HALF AN HOUR. IT KEEPS FOR UP TO 3 DAYS AFTER LAYERING AND BEFORE BAKING. CONVENIENT, TASTY, ECONOMICAL.

MEGADARRA: BOIL A PACK OF BROWN BASMATI RICE. BOIL HALF A BAG OF BROWN LENTILS. FRY TWO LOTS OF ONIONS – THE FIRST, CHOPPED SMALL IN LOTS OF OLIVE OIL, SO THAT YOU CAN MIX YOUR RICE AND LENTILS IN AMONG THEM, SALTED AND PEPPERED TO TASTE. THE SECOND, SLICE AND FRIED IN OLIVE OIL TILL FRAZZLED. PUT THE RICE, ONIONS AND LENTILS IN A WIDE DISH AND SCATTER THE FRAZZLED ONIONS OVER. IT TASTES DELICIOUS, MUCH BETTER THAN IT SOUNDS, SO GIVE IT A TRY. YOU COULD PROVIDE A NICE BOWL OF THICK YOGHURT ALONG WITH IT.

SLOW-ROASTED TOMATO SALAD WITH GOATS' CHEESE: THE NIGHT BEFORE, CUT A LARGE BATCH OF TOMATOES – FULL SIZE, NOT CHERRY – IN HALF ACROSS THEIR EQUATORS, AND LAY CUT-SIDE-UP IN A ROASTING TIN. DRIBBLE WITH OLIVE OIL, SCATTER WITH A LITTLE DRIED SAGE OR THYME OR ROSEMARY AND SOME SEA SALT AND BLACK PEPPER,

AND ROAST IN A HOT OVEN FOR 20 MINUTES. THEN SWITCH THE OVEN OFF AND LEAVE THEM IN OVERNIGHT. THEY COOK AND DRY OUT A BIT IN THE COOLING OF THE OVEN TO A SLIGHTLY CHEWY BUT STILL FRESH CONSISTENCY. PUT SOME SALAD LEAVES ON A BIG PLATTER, LAY OUT YOUR TOMATOES, THEN ROUGHLY TEAR UP SOME GOATS' CHEESE AND SCATTER OVER, ALONG WITH A FEW BLACK OLIVES IF YOU HAVE THEM.

CHAPTER 9: FORK AND BRIEFCASE

There was an extended period in my working life when I got lots of opportunities to do short jobs abroad. This was the era of EU membership and educational exchange programmes, sharing learning across frontiers and cultures. How I loved it. I know there's a lot to be cynical about ('gravy train,' I hear you mutter), and perhaps it wasn't always money 100% well spent. But personally, I embraced with joy the opportunity to experience things from a different angle, and it definitely helped me understand the world better. I would like to think I also contributed something to global wisdom, peace or whatever, in a modest way. And that's the last of the apologies! I had a blast.

My first ever trip was to Brussels for a week, helping represent a women-into-management course to which I'd contributed as a mentor. What joy! I was pinching myself in disbelief that I'd been chosen for this junket. Four of us took turns at looking after our stall – it wasn't arduous – and spent the rest of the time jollying around and seeing the sights. I visited the Bruegel and Tintin museums, and did a tour of 'social and historic Brussels'. This was fascinating – we think of Brussels as a bureaucratic centre and if pushed we might remember beer and Brussels sprouts.

However it's an old industrial city too, and our tour focused on the challenges to the workers over the centuries. They showed us a magnificent statue of coalminers, which portrayed women underneath, labouring around the plinth and supporting the weight of the industrial revolution on their shoulders. This reminded me of reading Zola's 'Germinal' when I was doing French at Uni – set in the north European coalfields of the 1860s. The miners went on strike, and the novel describes the harshness of the conflict, and women's place in the struggle for justice. Zola's account of how the women took revenge on the shop-keeper who refused them credit is eye-watering.

I was surprised at how elegant, and how French-influenced, the food in Brussels was. Until then I'd thought of Brussels as a dull city with no culture but plenty bureaucracy. But the café scene was a delight, with canal-side terraces and mature black-aproned waiters hefting spectacular platters of oysters and trays of Kir among the chattering tables. There was also Belgian chocolate from Leonidas – big fat, smooth, bittersweet delights. Quite a lot of them found their way home with me as gifts – we had nothing like them in Scotland at that time. It was their size as well as their unctuousness that made them so good. For a country girl, one of those after your meal nudged at the orgasmic. (As I write this story some 25 years later, we are in the process of trying to leave the European Union, and it's been a horrible, frustrating affair. Those who voted to leave will probably read this and think we should never have joined in the first place! I wish I'd made it back to Brussels for another visit before now, but I guess they'll still let us visit; deal or no deal.)

A year or so after Brussels, I found myself in Oporto, with a team from Dundee University, on another European-funded programme. I was with Denis, my boss, who was a vegetarian, and a couple of other colleagues. Not for the first time I found myself in the front line as official taster for the Scottish team, who were all a lot more timid about trying 'new stuff' than I was. Tripe was especially nauseating for my colleagues; but I rather liked the way they cooked it – savoury with tomatoes and garlic, rather than milky and stodgy as per my mother's version. On another occasion we were taken to a magnificent seafood restaurant by the Atlantic's crashing waves, and served with vast sharing platters of assorted crustaceans. We were each served a toolbox-worth of implements to crack and whack our way into the sweet, ocean-scented meat. It was delicious but unexpectedly exhausting – my hands were sore before my belly was satisfied.

Portugal was a particular challenge back then (mid 1990s) for a vegetarian, and our generous hosts were puzzled and a bit embarrassed about how to feed Denis. Eventually they uncovered a little vegetarian café in the maze of streets under the massive two-level bridge that crosses the Douro. In grateful relief, Denis fell with gusto on the tabbouleh and spinach and chickpeas; and this time it was the hosts who were struggling with how to feed themselves. Being an adventurous omnivore is such a useful thing in life, I have discovered over and over again. My mother's assaults with sago and overboiled cabbage have left me with no fears.

Our meetings and workshops in Oporto were held in a centre for people with cerebral palsy, and there was an excellent self-service canteen which catered for all the staff and centre members. We had a nice range of meaty stews with veggies and salads – home-cooked in style and very tasty – and there was also a little *pichet* of wine if you wanted it. All very civilised. On our second-last day there was a chicken dish on the menu, and Mina, one of our Portuguese colleagues, warned me that I might not like it, as it was a very traditional recipe. I asked what was in it, already reaching for a portion – 'traditional recipe' is an instant winner for me. 'The chicken is cooked in its own blood,' she replied. This was okay by me – black pudding being a regular back home – so I ate up and found it deliciously dark in flavour. Mina asked me if I would make this dish when I returned home, and I joked that this might bring on a divorce, as Bernard was by no means as adventurous a diner as me. 'Anyway,' I added, 'I wouldn't be able to buy the blood back home.'

'You can't buy blood?' She looked at me as if I was mad. 'What do you mean, you can't buy blood?'

Well I wasn't sure why – health and safety probably – but I was pretty sure that chicken blood was not available in your average British butcher's. I asked her how it was bought in Portugal – fresh or frozen? By the litre or processed into little stock cube thingies? She said she would take me to the market and show me.

Next day as promised, we were off to market – just Mina and me, as the others were away buying Porto United football shirts and records of Portuguese folk music to take home. European food markets? I could live in them. This one was vibrant and noisy and perfumed unmistakeably with meat; live hens and rabbits in hutches awaited their fate alongside the vast butcher's counters. Mina showed me the (unrefrigerated) chicken stall: rows of chickens at one end of the counter, and trays of solid brown gunk at the other. The gunk looked a bit like raw chocolate, although you wouldn't expect to see raw chocolate in such vast quantities; but of course it wasn't chocolate, it was dried blood. Women in the queue were buying it by the quarter-kilo to go with their nice fresh hen. 'Look up,' said Mina. Dangling from the crossbar were a line of naked chickens each with a poly bag of fresh, liquid, jewel-bright blood tied to its ankle. This, said Mina, was the gourmet option. What a shame not to be able to take some home after all.

Denis in due course moved on to another job, and I fell unexpectedly into a trip to Romania, taking his place. Dundee University had an exchange programme with a University in Cluj, Transylvania, and it was Dundee's turn to send someone to teach some stuff about community care. I was given travel information on the back of an envelope, and some advice on what kind of presents to take people (whisky; shortbread; nice quality soaps) for the generous hospitality I would be offered, along with some vague comments about the new regime. This was the mid-90s, just a few years after the fall of Ceausescu and the end of the Soviet regime; and the main news that had come out of Romania in those days was the discovery of vast numbers of orphanages where disabled children were routinely dumped, away from their families and in terrible conditions. The reports were horrifying. Off I went, excited and naïve as always.

Just getting to Cluj was an education in itself, especially as I was travelling alone. I arrived at Bucharest airport and had to manoeuvre my way through a complicated journey whose details I forget, to travel to Baneasa airport for my onward flight to Cluj. This regional airport was a bit of a shocker in the toilets department; shit-smeared and with blocked drains and no hand-washing facilities, my strong stomach was the only thing that saved me from certain Death by Diarrhoea. I'd seen plenty shit before, but not in an airport; it seemed the Romanians, on that day at least, had no regard for internal travellers or international relations. After a very uncomfortable wait at the airport, my flight was called and I boarded a dilapidated old plane that had clearly seen better days.

Some years earlier (1989) I'd gone on a tour with Dunfermline Abbey Choir to East Germany, and the plane back then had been old but severe and efficient, with lots of communist slogans in three languages (none of them English). I suppose in my naïve and uninformed way I expected Romanian planes to be the same. The Soviet world was shrouded in mystery.

The seat I'd been allocated to travel from Baneasa to Cluj had no safety belt. I looked around; the flight was full, and I could see that not everybody was using their safety belts anyway. I dithered a bit about whether to report this; communication felt suddenly very challenging, with no guarantee that English would be spoken or understood. I decided to leave it, and just travel hopefully; then couldn't face a flight that would start with me wilfully disobeying the routine injunction 'fasten your seatbelts please.' I imagined the five-year-old Harry being left motherless because his foolish mother had failed to report a non-functioning seatbelt. So I made a last-minute lurch for the safe option, and was moved to the only free seat, right at the back of the plane, on the aisle. From here, as we were taking off into the skies, I could hear the bustling of the crew in their little catering space right behind me. I looked over my shoulder to see the stewards crouching on the floor laying polystyrene cups out on a tray slanting strongly to diagonal, slittering in hot coffee. Then they were off up the aisle, handing out the drinks to stoic passengers. Of course I got splashed, but I was saying nothing. I drank the coffee, crossed my fingers, and prayed for a safe arrival.

In Cluj, I was accommodated in a staff hostel which was clean and tidy, if basic. Think Travelodge without a refurb budget. Breakfast was the only meal provided; there was a telephone kiosk just down the street, for which a plastic money card had to be purchased; there was a tram stop about a hundred yards away; there weren't any staff on view although there must have been some. I was told this was a 'hotel for visiting professors,' and it was clearly the best accommodation on offer. There was nothing wrong with it except that I couldn't figure out how to achieve a sense of calm. There were too many unknowns, and I spoke no Romanian, and nobody there spoke English, and my French and German were useless, and worst of all I was alone. I discovered that my optimism and courage melted like 'snaw aff a dyke', as my mother would have said, without a travelling companion to check things out with.

The staff at the university were very hospitable, and for three nights running, I was invited to dine with the families of each of the three female lecturers. It was great to see how people lived, and to be welcomed hospitably. The lecturers, despite having trained in the communist era where travel was strictly controlled, were fluent in several languages including English, and had indeed travelled widely. They lived in multi-storey blocks of graffiti-clad flats on the far edges of the city, with very little space and obviously no spare cash for domestic accoutrements. But they were generous and kind and fed me with local food and happily answered all my questions and plied me with lots of questions in return. They were living through a time of massive change; in the Soviet era, they had endured food shortages and travel restrictions and enforced pregnancy checks, as Ceausescu strove to build a huge population. If they, as women, didn't produce their allotted four children each they had to pay extra taxes. Any children born with infirmities or disabilities, and who survived, were removed to the newly-infamous orphanages. Now, in the 1990s, they were having to engage with different values and they had been told that entrepreneurialism was the way forward; but for a people previously rewarded for informing on each other, nobody trusted any kind of government official, and those who were trying to set up businesses in the brave new world were treated with deep suspicion. All of this I pieced together as these hard-working women took me into their homes after a busy day at work. I know there were huge gaps in my understanding but my European colleagues gave me a close-up view of life in that place, at those times, that most other visitors would have been denied, and that was an immense privilege.

I have two memories of the food they gave me. Memories of the first night's actual meal, with petite, worried and hard-working Doina, are lost in my sense of culture shock. However I do remember her story about a previous lecturer coming over from Dundee, and while Doina was serving the meal, someone on the ground floor of the tower block had decided to kill a pig. The pig's screams had been excruciating, and Doina's visitor quite taken aback – as I would have been. But killing a pig at the foot of a multi-storey block was apparently quite common, as Doina had tried to explain to her shocked guest.

On the second night, Andreea, a younger lecturer, took me home and gave me an evening meal with her husband and two primary-school-age children. None of them had much in the way of English but they tried their best and of course I was unable to help except through gestures. I found the food stodgy and greasy; there was a kind of dumpling and a kind of spam-fritter-like thing. For dessert they had bought ice lollies and the children were very excited about this, clearly it was a rare treat. I know this sounds ungrateful, but I wasn't. I'm just trying to be faithful in my reporting. After the meal, they took me out in their old Dacia to drive into the Transylvanian mountains, and told me of bears and picnics and long treks through the snow. It was stunning, very like the highest parts of Scotland but even higher, and deeply, darkly forested. The Dracula story was thin on my repertoire but howling wolves and thunderstorms were written into the very flanks of the mountains, even on a Spring evening.

The third evening meal I was treated to was very different. Ilinca was a little older, with perfect English, and rather elegant in her appearance. She spoke willingly, almost urgently, about the challenge of the past and her hopes for the present. It was she who described the fertility laws to me. She and her husband had defied the four-children rule; they were content with just the one, whom I met – a sprightly, clever eight-year-old – and were obliged to pay taxes for the three phantom children whom they refused to produce. However, she also spoke of the travel opportunities which were available to the workers if you qualified in various ways. Ilinca had managed to visit California, and had been dazzled by the display of beautiful fruits and vegetables in the open markets. Romania, she reminded me, had been known at one time as 'the bread basket of Europe,' and even in her day there were peasants who had managed to keep control of a small parcel of land, and tended orchards and grew wonderful vegetables. California's market stalls were a million times bigger – but she was bitterly disappointed in the flavour of the peaches she bought. Peaches she knew from home were sweet and perfumed and musky and juicy; her Californian peach was oversized and watery by comparison.

As we spoke, Ilinca set on the table a little dish with a cream-coloured sort of paste in it – maybe the texture of porridge. I didn't recognise it, and she showed me how to spread it on the lovely chewy bread she had provided. The flavour was deep and smoky with a garlicky depth and a greeny herby finish, the mouth-feel cool and smooth and light. I loved it but I still couldn't place it. She told me it was an aubergine puree, made with an extra aubergine she had cooked over a barbecue the previous summer, and then frozen to keep for a 'special occasion' – I was humbled. The smoking, she said, was key to the flavour – you could make the dish with an unsmoked aubergine and it would still be good, but not this good. I had never come across Baba Ganoush or the French Caviar d'Aubergines at that stage, and I was hooked. And deeply impressed by her household economy talents; like me, she was a thrifty gourmet. But I had a lot more to learn than she did.

The shop shelves in Cluj were pretty bare. I bought some teabags and a few biscuits for my room in the hostel, but the items I looked out for – those that would say 'Romania' when I took them back home as gifts – weren't apparent. Cluj is a beautiful old city with streets that reminded me of Paris; spared the worst excesses of Communist reprogramming, there are magnificent old buildings from the renaissance, baroque and gothic periods. I wandered around enjoying the scenery but the language barrier, and being alone, sucked at my courage. I needed a cup of tea – but cafes were hidden behind closed doors, and I lacked the resolve to push one of them open and figure out the local etiquette. Not so much of an international traveller after all; I felt discouraged. I rounded a corner and came upon a bunch of workmen in striped work clothes digging a hole in the ground. They immediately triggered a memory of a shocking photo I'd seen of Jews in a concentration camp in Nazi Germany; it took my breath away. Were they prisoners doing community service, or forced labour? Surely no government would debase its workmen in clothes so unswervingly reminiscent of the Nazi regime? I found myself scarpering in the opposite direction, quite unnerved. Then I came upon a gypsy lady dressed in brilliant colours, selling pretzels on the street; she saved me. Her pretzels were the size of soup plates, bronzed and salted, and they were accessible to me, for a few pennies, right there on the street with no closed doors to negotiate. I kept the warm paper bag till I was on the tram home, and couldn't wait any longer for a wee morsel. It felt like the entire tramload of passengers was watching me dig my fingers into the bag and lift the delicious bread to my lips; then they would all look away as soon as they realised I'd clocked them. I decided not to care; the pretzels were chewy and bready and absolutely delicious, and restored my morale for the time being.

I was there to do some teaching on the (then) new Community Care regime in the UK, and was keen to do so; but of course it was difficult given the language barriers. The translator and I struggled to explain foreign concepts such as 'voluntary organisation', one of the key components of community care legislation. Rows of polite students sat quietly staring at me, clearly understanding not a jot.

Some of the Masters students were deployed to translate; I had already met a couple of them when they had come on a previous exchange visit to Dundee. On one of the days, Florin was to escort me across town to a different building used by the University, and we chatted as we went. He was maybe 22 years old, young and bursting with enthusiasm for all the opportunities opening up to him through the fall of communism and his clever brain. As we were strolling along the streets, he spied half a dozen lettuces on a market stall and asked if I would mind waiting a moment. Transformed from excited young careerist to vigilant householder, he poked critically among the lettuces, picked one up, examined it carefully, sniffed it, and finally put it back down on the stall and turned away. 'Aren't you going to buy it?' I asked, somewhat mystified. He replied that he thought he could get a better one at another market elsewhere in the town. I've never met any other 22-year-old young man who took so seriously the purchase of a lettuce. I guessed it was all about the shortages; and trying to retain standards.

Yet another Masters student, Violeta, took me to the flat she shared with her boyfriend. Her grandparents were peasants with a little bit of land, and Violeta described them and their setting and skills with great pride. She insisted on giving me a bottle of her grandmother's home-made *ţuica* – a distilled spirit made from plums. I'd already tasted it and must have made appreciative comments. It was definitely firewater; or 'blaw yer heid aff' as we'd say back home. I lugged the litre bottle all the way back through the two airports and Customs, and found nobody back home would drink it more than once!

Ilinca, Florin and Violeta taught me all I ever need to know about food and cooking: make the very best you can with whatever humble produce you have at hand, and don't be taken in by the flashy stuff that others might value. Use your eyes, nose and other senses to choose what is good. Honour your ancestors for their skills and knowledge. Be proud of your heritage and open to learning from others. Be generous.

A PIE FOR ALL SEASONS

WE'RE VERY FOND OF A PIE IN SCOTLAND. ANY KIND OF PIE. A WEE HAND-HELD SCOTCH PIE CAN VARY FROM CHEAP AND CHEERFUL TO DEEPLY SAVOURY; A BIG BUTCHERS' STEAK PIE IS A FAVOURITE FOR BRINGING IN THE NEW YEAR. IT'S PARTLY THE PASTRY THAT DOES IT. NOBODY, EVEN ME, MAKES PUFF PASTRY FROM SCRATCH NOWADAYS. WHY WOULD YOU WHEN YOU CAN BUY SUCH GOOD STUFF READY-MADE? THE BUTTERY FLAKINESS MAKES YOU HAPPY BEFORE YOU'VE EVEN REACHED THE FILLING. HOWEVER IT'S A BIT CALORIE-LADEN AND I LIKE TO MAKE A PIE WITH MASHED POTATO ON TOP INSTEAD OF PASTRY, ONCE IN A WHILE. MY PARTNER COMPLAINS WHEN I DO THIS AS HE SAYS IT'S NOT A REAL PIE. WELL, I BEG TO DIFFER.

WHAT TO PUT INSIDE YOUR PIE? ANYTHING YOU LIKE, REALLY. IT CAN BE MEAT OR FISH OR VEGETARIAN; SAVOURY OR SWEET. I'VE MADE SOME GOOD VEGETARIAN FILLINGS WITH RED PEPPERS, SPINACH AND CREAM CHEESE; OR CHICK PEAS, SPICES, ONIONS AND CARROTS. I'VE MADE SOME SPECIAL 'PROJECT' PORK PIES WITH HOT WATER CRUST PASTRY AND REAL GELATINE MADE BY BOILING UP A PIG'S TROTTER. I'VE DONE A RANGE OF RICH BEEF CASSEROLES WITH PUFF PASTRY ON TOP, SO EASY. AND LOADS OF SHEPHERD'S PIES WITH BEEF MINCE AND

A CROWN OF MASHED POTATO. PROBABLY MY FAVOURITE IS A FISH PIE, ESPECIALLY IF I NEED SOMETHING BIG TO FEED LOTS OF PEOPLE.

TAKE CARE WITH YOUR WHITE SAUCE, WHICH YOU WILL NEED TO BIND YOUR FILLING. USE TWO OR THREE DIFFERENT TYPES OF FISH AND MAKE SURE ONE OF THEM IS SMOKED, SO THAT WHEN YOU POACH THE FISH IN THE MILK, THE LOVELY SMOKY FLAVOUR COMES THROUGH. AND MAKE SURE YOUR FISH IS SUSTAINABLY SOURCED AS WELL. INCLUDE SOME BAY LEAVES AND PEPPERCORNS AND PARSLEY STALKS IN YOUR POACHING LIQUID. MAKE SURE YOUR SAUCE IS THICK ENOUGH. A FEW PRAWNS GO QUITE WELL, AS DOES HARD-BOILED EGG IN MODERATION. KEEP YOUR MASHED POTATO QUITE LOOSE AND CREAMY, WITH LOTS OF BUTTER AND MILK, AND CHOPPED PARSLEY IN MY VIEW TRANSFORMS IT – ALTHOUGH YOU MIGHT DISAGREE.

THAT'S ALL YOU'RE GETTING BY WAY OF A RECIPE. AWAY AND EXPERI-MENT. IF YOU JUST PAY ATTENTION TO WHAT YOU'RE DOING, IT'LL TASTE GREAT AND YOUR FRIENDS WILL BE HAPPY. IF YOU HAVE LEFT-OVERS, YOU CAN MASH THE WHOLE THING TOGETHER NEXT DAY, AND MAKE BRILLIANT FISHCAKES.

DON'T WASTE ANYTHING. TOO MANY FISHERMEN HAVE DIED AT SEA FOR THAT. AND WE KEEP HEARING THAT IN OUR OWN LIFETIMES, FISH WILL DISAPPEAR FROM OUR DIET BECAUSE OF OUR NEGLECT OF THE PLANET. SO LET'S RESPECT IT, AND ENJOY IT WHILE WE CAN.

CHAPTER 10: HARMONY IN HOSPITALITY

A few more years down the line, and with some research experience under my belt, I happened to be in the right place at the right time for a small freelance job that nobody else wanted. This was another European project, aimed at 'harmonising' qualifications across EU member countries, in the field of hospitality and tourism. The aspiration was that workers in hospitality and tourism could move easily across Europe and have their qualifications recognised. This would clearly be of personal value to those workers who wanted to travel round a bit. However, for the industry itself it would be a major advantage: these industries rely heavily on untrained labour and pay low wages even when people manage to gain a few qualifications. Many of the biggest multinational companies need to be able to set up in new countries and quickly train their staff to minimum standards; and it's helpful if they can move their senior staff around easily to train up new workforces. Across Europe, tourism contributes hugely to national economies – including in Scotland, which just goes to show it's not all about sunshine.

This new project involved partners from the Further Education sectors in Finland, France, Austria, Italy, England and Scotland, from a range of Hospitality and Tourism (or HoT, as we soon named the project) disciplines. It was my task to collate and analyse statistics and 'soft' data to accompany the production of harmonisation-directed learning materials. And meetings would be held in every country involved in the project! Once again, I couldn't believe my luck.

Up till then I hadn't really worked in the hospitality and tourism sectors, so I was able to gain a rapid, if patchy, insight into some aspects of the industry. In my romantic naivete I hadn't really thought much about how this massive industry is organised, and my understanding was limited to what the Sunday paper travel supplements had to say about beach holidays in the Maldives or city tours in Prague. There were many revelations for me. I volunteered to proofread and edit the learning materials as they were developed and that gave me a smattering of theoretical understanding too. The marketing module, for instance, was an eye-opener, and utterly fascinating.

From a food perspective, we ate as guests in the student restaurants run by all the colleges represented in the partnership. I had worked in a Scottish college for a number of years, and my friend Sheila from the Abbey choir headed up the school of Hospitality and Tourism there. We used to whisper-gossip about recipes and methods and so on during the Sunday morning sermons, while waiting to sing the Agnus Dei; so I was no stranger to the broad outline of the curriculum, or indeed to student restaurants. These were always very popular among staff – high quality food at discounted prices, with a smidgeon of fine-dining ambience. Just a smidgeon, though. Some students took to hospitality like ducks to water and could smile and serve their way through a challenging four-course menu and a bunch of fussy customers without faltering one iota. Others though – well – I have a vivid memory one Christmas season of a student-waiter giving in to exasperation at a hungry student's request for extra bread: 'you're just a bloody nuisance!' he snapped. Oops, you could see his chances of passing going down the drain. Still, it was intriguing to see how student restaurants functioned in other countries.

Italy provided my best memory of a student restaurant. My journey there, however, was a bit on the eventful side.

I'd been to Florence before – briefly – and I wanted to go back. There were various routes to my final destination in Città di Castello, in Umbria, including one through Florence. *Firenze!* The romance of it! I would have to get a train from Florence to Arezzo and then a taxi. The other routes, through Rome and other desirable places, weren't any more direct, as Città di Castello is somewhat off the beaten track. And Florence had the advantage over Rome of being small; so maybe the transfer would be easier. Or so I thought.

I was travelling alone; the others for various reasons had chosen their own routes and timescales. My flight was to leave Edinburgh midday, for Amsterdam, and from there I would catch the Florence flight. But for reasons uncertain – I think there was a big fire, or an explosion, or some other unnatural disaster in Amsterdam – the first leg of my flight was considerably delayed.

Eventually I arrived six hours late in Florence. It was 10.30pm, pitch dark, and the airport was closing. In my usual thrifty manner I looked for the bus into town, but it seemed the buses had finished for the day. I was nervous of the taxi rank; all those powerful engines and their nonchalant, watchful drivers hanging around smoking, eyeing up the fares as they shambled into view, tired and stressed by their journeys. I walked round the airport again, looking for an information desk; but it too was closed. The place was all but deserted. There was a cleaner; but she didn't speak English and my Italian vocabulary took me nowhere. I peered more carefully at the bus timetable; but I couldn't understand it. And there was a complete absence of buses.

Reluctantly I approached the taxi rank. Not so many taxis now but still somehow a sense of menace. I reminded myself that this was probably just a cultural miscommunication and stepped up to the first in the queue. I told the driver I needed to get to the railway station and he agreed, and put my suitcase in the boot. I was climbing in the back of the car when I saw that he had been approached by another driver, and they were in deep discussion. 'Go with him,' said my first driver, depositing my luggage back on the ground. Without a common language I didn't know how to question this. Why was I to change to another taxi? Well, it could just have been so that the first man could go home to his loving wife and/or ailing child and/or to watch the football on the telly. I had no way of finding out. I spoke to the second driver and repeated that I wanted to go to the railway station.

'Where are you travelling to from the station?' he enquired. His English was broken and accented but he obviously had some knowledge of my home language.

'Arezzo. Then on to Città di Castello.'

From the corner of my eye I could see that all the other drivers were climbing into their cars and driving away into the night. It was just me and the new driver.

'The station will be closed at this time of night.'

'But I looked up the timetable and I know there are trains to Arezzo.'

'There have been problems with the railways today. It is closed.'

Oh boy. What next? 'Please take me to the station so that I can check. And then if the trains are off, to a hotel where I can stay for the night.' He shrugged and put my case in his boot. He took off towards the city centre – that golden casket of mediaeval masterpieces, the city I longed to stroll around and absorb. Tonight it was dark as pitch and Michelangelo's David was nowhere to be seen. My driver paused in front of a station building which certainly looked quiet, though not exactly deserted. 'See,' he said, 'closed.' How was I to know what a closed railway station would look like in the far-off and legendary city of the artists?

'Let me go and check,' I said, my hand on the door handle.

'I could take you to Città di Castello,' he suggested.

'But it's such a long way! I couldn't possibly afford it,' I replied.

'You will pay a fortune for a hotel bed in Firenze. You know, this is a very expensive city. And then you won't arrive till halfway through tomorrow. I can get you there tonight.'

There was some sense in this argument. 'How much would you charge to take me to Città di Castello?' I asked.

'400 euros.'

'400 euros! No, just leave me here at the station.'

'You would not be safe. You will pay 400 euros for a hotel, if you can find one. Everywhere is booked up. And then you would still have to pay for your train fare and taxi from Arezzo.'

I could feel my head going light, my throat drying up. What I imagine high blood pressure might feel like, although to my knowledge I have never suffered such a thing. 'I don't have 400 euros on me.'

'I will take you to an ATM and you can get the money.'

It felt like my options were closing in. I wasn't very keen on this man, but what would it be like to be left alone in the middle of a dark, foreign city, not knowing my way round and with nowhere to stay the night? It was already close to midnight. I puffed out a breath and said, 'Okay. 400 euros. Città di Castello.' We went to an ATM, I drew out the money I needed for the fare, and we headed off.

The driver hit the motorway south. He speeded up, and speeded up again. The back seat was quite spacious but not especially comfortable, and I held tight to the door handle to avoid being bounced around like a cork. We raced down the motorway, ever faster. Two or three times he drove up close by another car and wound his window down, gesturing to the other driver to do likewise. Two or three shouted conversations took place at maybe 80 miles an hour, in which the driver seemed to be asking for directions. He didn't seem to know where Città di Castello was.

His driving grew more and more erratic and I started to feel sick. I peered to try to read the speedometer, and as I was doing so, noticed that his fare counter was running – and the price was getting higher. Already over 300 euros. Had he forgotten that we had agreed the fare? I decided to wait till the end of the journey before challenging him on this, which was a pity because then he would have a counted comparison to make. But then, I reasoned, he should never have agreed a fare for a place he clearly didn't even know how to find.

I felt nauseous from the lurching of the car. I closed my eyes and clung to the seat and prayed for the journey to be over. How was this nightmare journey going to end? I imagined myself raped and left in a ditch. Or just abandoned without my luggage. Place names were flashing by on the overhead gantries and I recognised 'Arezzo'. So probably we were going in the right direction. Another hour passed and there was a sign for Città di Castello. Thank goodness. I thought I might explode with tension. The driver screeched off the motorway and into town, searching for the city centre. 'Which hotel?' he shouted at me over his shoulder, and weakly I summoned my memory and told him. Maybe we were actually going to reach the right place. My next challenge would be to retrieve my luggage before telling him he wasn't getting the 600-odd euros which the fare counter now registered. I thought he would want to be paid before he let me out of the car. He slewed onto the pavement in front of my hotel and rammed on the breaks. I staggered out of the back seat, nearly collapsing on my knees. He opened the boot and slammed my bag on the ground. Thank goodness!

'650 euros.'

I felt on stronger ground now. '400 was what we agreed.'

He glared at me. 'You are mistaken.'

I clutched at my suitcase. 'You said 400. That's all I have, and that's all you're getting.'

He ranted at me in Italian, waving his fist and I squared my shoulders. 'You said 400.' I can be as obstinate as the best of them, and I do hate being taken advantage of. How dare he? '400 euros,' I repeated. He stormed into the hotel lobby and a sleepy concierge appeared behind the desk. The driver launched into a long and impassioned story, gesturing at me, and clearly describing me as a no-good cheating bitch of a tourist who wouldn't pay her fare. I interrupted and told the concierge, in English, that this driver had quoted me one fare and now wanted far more, and that he had driven like a maniac, and that I certainly wasn't paying more than the agreed 400 euros. The driver bellowed for a bit longer and the concierge looked pretty anxious. He summoned up some English: 'you pay now, we see manager tomorrow.'

'I haven't got 650 euros! And even if I had …'

His hands were hovering over the till. 'Call the manager!' I shouted. The driver ranted again. 'Call the police!' I shrieked. The driver waved his fist. The concierge opened the till, pulled out a wad of notes, and handed them to the driver. 'Don't do it!' I hollered. The driver flicked me the V sign, stuffed the notes in his pocket and stormed out. He gunned the taxi into life again and headed north. My nightmare journey was over. I was weak with exhaustion and now, of course, discovered I was ravenously hungry.

I got a sandwich. I got keys for a room. I phoned home. I went to bed shaking. The next day I met up with my colleagues and our Italian hostess took me to the police station to make a statement. In English, which she translated, and they typed up and got me to sign. Bloody hell. I thought at the time that they must be horrified that the reputation of their lovely country, city and town should be so besmirched by such a dreadful event. Alas, it seems they just thought I was mad to refuse to pay the inflated fare. Maybe. Maybe not. I was damned if I was going to be bullied.

You may say, it's only money. Not worth fighting over. You may be right but it's not my way.

ANYWAY, back to the college restaurant. We – a group of about eight of us, from the member countries' colleges – were being hosted by our partners in the hill town of Città di Castello. The training restaurant was lofty and elegant, lit softly by long shuttered windows and muslin curtains. The front-of-house students were decked out in formal black and white and the silver cutlery glittered in rows on either side of one's place. The linen was stiffened to perfection. In the middle of the heavy round wooden table sat a massive platter of fruit – each piece burnished invitingly, like one of those Dutch still lives you see in the Kelvingrove Museum, all glistening quinces and pomegranates. Claudette, one of our Edinburgh colleagues, entering into the languorous spirit of the occasion, reached out and plucked a massive shining grape from the bunch. 'Stop!' gasped our Italian hostess. 'Don't eat it!' Too late; Claudette bit, sucked and swallowed – looked puzzled, then retched into her starched napkin. Here was a new thing for me to learn; in Italy, and who knows where else, it is the custom to buff your centrepiece fruit display with furniture polish. And not the custom, as a diner, to reach out and eat it!

Our Italian hostesses took us to lovely little local restaurants where we ate squid-ink pasta and polenta with mushrooms, teaching us the difference between *antipasti* and *primi/secondi piatti, contorni* and *dolce*. Dishes were delivered to your table with a simple portion of whatever it was you had ordered – nothing was dressed up or adorned with extra bits and pieces. But the quality of the ingredients, and the cooking of them, was superb. One of the lecturers owned a vineyard which produced a lovely Montepulciano d'Abruzzo; this seemed to me like the last word in rustic sophistication. I could have very happily stayed in Città di Castello for a year, maybe two, maybe ten, just learning about food and drink and taste at the table.

In Vienna we rode around the ring of the city in tramcars and were driven out of town to wine and bier kellers. Descending back into the city through winding roads in the dark, lights twinkling and magnificent public buildings dramatically floodlit, was magical. It was like leafing through a book of chocolate-box covers, every vista so perfectly kitsch. Food was robust, and cakes were the big thing: we were given Mohnkuchen – a moist, spongy sort of cake which, if your eyes were closed, you'd have imagined to be pale yellow in colour; but it was strangely black. '*Mohne*' were the key ingredient – poppy seeds. I quite liked it – to Scottish eyes it was a bit of a curiosity, but it wasn't too sweet, and the texture was pleasantly gritty. In my overheated imagination, it was a metaphor for the city itself – despite its prettiness, who could tell what lurked behind closed doors? I visited the

Belvedere museum to see the Klimts – astonishingly decorative, golden, ravishing, urgent paintings of lovers embracing. And also of calm pastoral landscapes, houses, forests – I preferred these actually – they would have been easier to live with, evoking a gentle sense of home, peace and security.

Vienna is famous for her coffee shops – vast tea rooms glittering with art deco mirrors and fine china, lace doilies and silver cake forks. It seems they were frequented, in the early 20th century, by intellectuals, artists and radicals of the day. Again I was on my own when I tried these out, and felt intimidated rather than charmed. I remember writing to Marian saying I wished she was with me – together we'd have done justice to a Viennese coffee house.

I visited the Freud Museum – home and consulting rooms of Sigmund Freud, the originator of psychoanalysis. There were extracts in glass cases from his major case studies, including the famous Dora, and the couch she lay on for her confessions. Sorry – consultations! It's tempting for me to dismiss the experience as a bit spooky, but that would be lazy. Through the years I'd read bits of the history of psychoanalysis, and although Freud has been discredited to a large extent, I believe his contribution to understanding human nature was massive. He insisted on the importance of the unconscious in trying to understand and inter-pret apparently dysfunctional behaviour; and exposed the traumas experienced throughout life by victims of sexual abuses, including incest. Visiting the museum was quite a sobering experience, but an important one.

Soon after Harry's birth I'd taken a part-time job in the sheriff court in Dunfermline, and one morning had a brief conversation with one of the defence lawyers. I'd mentioned that the Abbey Choir was looking into the possibility of a tour to Vienna (which sadly never came off). 'Vienna!' he spat. 'Protecting all those Nazis!' It seemed that many Nazis had taken refuge, along with their stolen artworks, in Vienna following the end of the Second World War and were being protected by various influential networks. In my curiosity one day I asked one of our hosts about this, and was met by a shocked, embarrassed silence and an immediate change of subject. I guess I'd touched on a sore point. Tact isn't always my top virtue. I wanted to learn about the world, and what better opportunity than working abroad and meeting 'real' citizens – as opposed to the range of front-of-house people you normally meet as a tourist? I'd assumed, wrongly, that my colleagues would feel the same way and be comfortable in entering into this kind of conversation. Looking back, I can't decide whether I was just being completely raw, gauche, and insensitive – or whether my Austrian colleague was being defensive and stiffly formal. Politics are, of course, a minefield, and not my strong point. But that doesn't stop me wanting to know what life is like for the citizens of Elsewhere.

The other surprising thing I learned about Vienna was that it had been temporarily partitioned immediate after the war in the same way as Berlin, with American, British, French and Russian quarters. This little fact was dropped in during a 'historic tour' of the city which left me with more questions than answers. Carol Reed's 1949 film 'The Third Man', from the short story by Graham Greene, explores post-war Vienna and gives it an enduringly seedy, atmospheric, rather spooky ambience. At the time of my visit I had never seen the film and if I had, I wouldn't have recognised it – my experience was kitsch and curious rather than creepy.

In Finland, the tourism students of our partner college led us through a delightful evening of games and activities which helped us explore Finnish culture. Including a visit to the sauna. We ate muscular fish fresh from the Baltic, and learned that drinking alcohol in public places was restricted, attracting a certain degree of disapproval. At dinner, I sat beside a marketing manager who showed me photos of his massive motorbike, and of him doing wheelies in the snow. He told me about his motor-cycle travels around rural Finland and, aware of the long border between the two countries, I asked him if he had ever crossed into Russia. He fixed me with a glare and announced, 'I will never wolontarily go into Russia.' Then he told me about whole groups of Finnish people going missing during the Cold War era, and the ongoing hatreds of Finns for their near neighbours. I had never known.

Helsinki is clustered over a scatter of islands at the mouth of the river Vantaa, and it was strange and exciting to turn a corner in a city street and find yourself face to face with an ocean-going liner pulled up at the quayside. We visited the fish market, scented with salt and glittering with silvery pinky bluey trout and salmon and mackerel and cod and haddock, laid out on slabs under canvas canopies along the quayside. No doubt the main market business went on in the early mornings – by the time we got there it was just tourists and citizens hurrying home, picking up something *en route* to feed the family. I wished that was me, choosing a nice wee handful of herrings to feed my loved ones.

The main railway station nearby showed destinations for St Petersburg and Moscow, with further train/ferry options for Tallinn, Stockholm, Copenhagen, Amsterdam, Brussels and Paris. I remember thinking that an extended Baltic tour would make a fantastic adventure, should the opportunity ever come my way.

Our French partners, the college of the Accor hotel group, with-drew from the project early on; but I as researcher was required to go and interview them, to capture something of their training activities and their interest in transferability of learning across the EU. Their 'academy' was on the outskirts of Paris, and I got there by train. This was a fascinating visit; the Accor group has hotels all over the world, and the need for constant learning and relearning was an urgent reality for them. They spoke to me of cultural challenges to do with the religious and ethnic priorities of large groups of staff in low-paid jobs. They provided the front-line service for customers from vastly different backgrounds, generally much wealthier than the staff in question and with far greater life opportunities. Certain training requirements were fundamental and relatively easily achieved – e.g. food hygiene or health and safety – but it was much harder to engender a commitment to company values in settings where language barriers reinforced other feelings of isolation or even alienation. Our project in the 'harmonisation' of training systems, to be truly effective, would need to take these personnel fundamentals of the industry into account.

My head jostling with insights generously imparted by my hosts, I made my way back into Paris and looked for somewhere to eat near my budget hotel. I was tired and needed a place where I could sit quietly alone and digest some of this rich material; I didn't want any main-street restaurant with an expectation of formality. I needed to slump a bit; and I was hungry; and after all this was Paris: so I wanted to eat well. I found a little back-street bistro with some outside tables and settled myself down. The menu was rustic and inviting – in particular, there was *choucroute garnie*, a cabbage and pork/ham combination which I'd heard Marian describe, with smacking lips. There was a word in the description of the dish – *jarret* – which I didn't recognise, so I asked the waitress to explain. She was a mature woman, wiry and strong and probably nearer 60 than 50. She hitched up her black skirt and pointed to her knee – 'genou', she said – and of course I understood immediately – what we would call the pig's knuckle. So I ordered the choucroute, along with a half-litre *pichet* of house red, and in due course it arrived. An enormous platter of pickled cabbage with lots of different kinds of pork and ham – absolutely magnificent in a peasanty sort of way, meant for sharing and despite my valiant efforts to leave a clean plate, just too big. But so delicious.

Back home in Dunfermline, I was involved as a volunteer with a local day centre for older people, and we wanted to provide an opportunity for staff in the voluntary sector to gain a broader perspective on their work. We had a contact in Greece; so we fundraised and managed to set up a week-long study tour for eight of us to go and see how older people's services are delivered in Greece. Part of our curiosity was in seeing how fit and healthy older people were, getting by on their simple and delicious Mediterranean diet – bread, olive oil, vegetables, fruit, salads, fish, and a little meat.

We visited a care home run by the Greek Orthodox Church – and were shown round by a solemn priest in full black habit with a tall hat and a long grey beard. He kept up a flowing commentary of the virtues of the place, referring more than once to the 'disgrace' that families had abandoned their parents to the care system. How shocking it was, he said, when it was a family's duty to care for their older relatives throughout life. Following us round was a small group of residents, hanging on his every word. I was cringing. How must it feel to them, I wondered, that their shameful 'abandonment' was being set forth as the source of the Church's mission? Our interpreter, Costas, an old-age psychologist, later explained to us that in Greece, more and more women were going out to work. Traditionally, women had done all the domestic and care work within families – but taking in an ageing relative was becoming too challenging on top of working life. Costas' own wife was now working, and it seemed that theirs was the first generation where this had become reasonably common, if not yet universal. He could see that systems would have to change in Greece, because it seemed unlikely that the women would ever choose to give up their new-found freedoms and opportunities to go back to the old ways.

This is the trend everywhere with the care of older people; Greece was a bit behind the UK in this respect, but not so very much. Progress for one group carries penalties for others. But

Costas told us that in his working life he had come across many old people supposedly being cared for by their families, who spent their days locked in bedrooms with no company and sometimes barely enough food and drink – perhaps because the families were too ashamed to ask for help. Or because supportive systems didn't exist.

Greek services for older people were at their best in their system of day centres. When you retired in Greece, you were given a membership of a day centre in the same way that we in the UK are given bus passes. The day centres were well funded, and provided a focus for whole ranges of activities for people at this very active, engaged stage of their lives. There were choirs and drama groups, arts and crafts, exercise programmes, holiday clubs, and everywhere, the traditional backgammon. Visiting the day centres was enlivening and inspiring. Men attended in the mornings and women in the afternoons. We asked one man why this was, and he replied without a shred of irony that his wife had to stay at home in the mornings to prepare his lunch!

We were invited to join the local 'parliament' discussion in which older people were required to be well represented. Here, policies for civic life were debated with vigour, with older people contributing passionately. They were ahead of us in this – back home at this time, efforts were being made to involve older people in shaping community care policies, rather than just being passive recipients of the end result; but then of course, democracy was invented in Greece and clearly they know how to make it happen.

International Day for Older People (1st October) was celebrated during our visit; in fact in setting up the trip, our Greek contacts had recommended that we choose our dates to coincide. They held a massive dinner with dancing afterwards, for 800 people, and us at the top table. The hall was ringing with conviviality as the courses were delivered to the tables – grilled vegetables and souvlaki (little lamb kebabs) and bread and olives, in plentiful quantities, with lots of red wine, and finishing off with ouzo. Some of the older people we had met on our visits were there and took charge of showing us how to perform the traditional Greek dances. Big circles, sideway steps and back again – it was bewildering. These oldies were fit, that was for sure. And their fitness must have come in handy when they had to go to the loo, as we discovered later on. No seats. Just a hole in the floor with a footplate on either side, and for us (rather younger) Scots at least, it proved very tricky indeed to avoid falling down the hole!

All of this took place nearly 20 years ago as I write; and there has been a fair bit of research in the meantime, exploring the anti-cancer properties of the so-called 'Mediterranean Diet'. There is some good evidence that a diet rich in vegetables and fruit, low in saturated fat, plenty oily fish and moderate amounts of red meat, and low in sugar, enhances your chances of living to a healthy old age. Interestingly, there is also some evidence that people benefit from conviviality at mealtimes. It's not just about what you eat, it's the whole experience of sitting down with the family or a group of friends, and sharing the day's experiences, that contributes to your wellbeing.

Amen to that.

A few years later, our day centre in Scotland organised another study tour – this time to the Netherlands. We were invited to visit an 800-bedded nursing home in Vlaardingen, near Rotterdam; and were fortunate that our visit coincided with Herring Day. Before I embark on an unseemly rush to describe the gustatory delights, let me just explain that we were highly suspicious of a nursing home of that size, feeling certain that it could not possibly provide any kind of quality personal care. In the UK at that time, all the old, massive institutions were closing in favour of small, more personal group living arrangements. In fact, what we found in Vlaardingen was that the nursing home occupied a large, well-designed site, with individual units built around a farm. The sheep were being shorn that day, and residents with varying levels of independence were coming out to watch the shearing. As people became frailer, they would move into more supported systems in the different units. Everywhere, there were opportunities for people to participate in activities like gardening and cooking, as well as leisure activities; and for those whose physical and mental frailty threatened to overwhelm them, there was high-input professional care. It wasn't perfect, but show me a place with a perfect system of caring for an ageing population? I think the Dutch, in their straightforward, egalitarian way, were trying to develop systems that were respectful as well as affordable. I found the staff, in my short visit, to be committed and kind.

Back to Herring Day, which celebrated the first catch of the season. At lunchtime, we were treated to a fabulous array of fresh raw fish, lightly cured. I had never tasted anything so delightful! Once again I saved our national reputation by being the only one of our party to relish such delicacies. Some of the others managed to taste one, smile and politely decline a second; unfortunately others wouldn't even try. I have never understood this attitude to food and particularly, to the hospitality of others. It embarrasses me. But hey, I do my best to make up for it! The herring was delicious.

One last job which afforded travel opportunities was with a small research company where we were trying to put together a case for European funding, and identified partners in the Netherlands. So I had a couple of trips to Amsterdam, Kampen and Utrecht, and later on my own, flying visits to Krakow and Prague, to meet with potential collaborators. Each of these visits had their own little culinary surprises and I had the great good fortune to be working with people who enjoyed my curiosity about their national cuisines and were happy to answer my questions. In that short trip I enjoyed Dutch pancakes, Polish dumplings and Czech beer. All good stuff.

I have found that I love travelling in a working context, to see how real people live – so much more satisfying than just going on holiday and being delivered a packaged experience. And how lucky to be given these opportunities.

BLACK IS BACK

MOHNKUCHEN WOULD BE AN UNUSUAL FEATURE ON A SCOTTISH TEA PLATE, BUT WE DO HAVE OTHER BLACK DAINTIES. CHIEF AMONG THESE IS THE FAMOUS BLACK BUN, A RICH FRUIT CAKE ENCASED IN PASTRY WHICH ONLY EVER APPEARS AT HOGMANAY. IT'S AN ENORMOUS, HEAVY, WEIGHTY AFFAIR BUT IT GOES DOWN VERY WELL WITH A WEE DRAM OF WHISKY, ESPECIALLY IF YOU'RE PLANNING TO PARTY ALL NIGHT. I ONCE MADE ONE TO TAKE ON A NEW YEAR BREAK TO KRAKOW. YOU MIGHT THINK THE KRAKOWIANS HAVE ENOUGH PROBLEMS OF THEIR OWN; BUT MY FRIEND LYNDA AND I WERE HEADING OFF THERE FOR A LONG WEEKEND, AND I MUST HAVE BEEN FEELING SLIGHTLY REGRETFUL NOT TO BE CELEBRATING NEW YEAR AT HOME. WE STOOD WITH CROWDS OF REVELLERS IN THE MAIN SQUARE IN KRAKOW, UNDER THE FIREWORKS, PASSING ROUND SLICES OF BLACK BUN AND SLURPING EACH OTHER'S DRINKS. IT WAS VERY FRIENDLY. WOULD I MAKE A TRADITIONAL BLACK BUN AGAIN? MAYBE ONLY FOR NOSTALGIA'S SAKE. I CAN JUST IMAGINE THE BIRDS SWOOPING IN FOR THE INEVITABLE WODGE OF LEFTOVERS.

THERE IS ANOTHER BLACK CAKE WHICH IS A LOT MORE MANAGEABLE, POPULARLY KNOWN AS 'FLY CEMETERY'. IT'S A KIND OF FRUIT SLICE, MADE MAINLY WITH CURRANTS SANDWICHED BETWEEN TWO LAYERS OF

CRISP SWEET PASTRY. MY AUNT CIS USED TO MAKE ONE EVERY SATURDAY AFTERNOON TO LINE THE STOMACHS OF 'THE MEN' GOING OUT TO THE PUB AT NIGHT (FRY-UP OF BACON, EGG AND SAUSAGE, BUTTERED ROLLS, LOADS OF TEA AND FLY CEMETERY. WHO SAYS SCOTS DON'T KNOW HOW TO DRINK RESPONSIBLY? MIND YOU, THAT WAS 50 YEARS AGO.)

I HAVE BEEN EXPERIMENTING AS IT HAS OCCURRED TO ME THAT FLY CEMETERY IS IN FACT JUST BLACK BUN MADE HANDY; AND AM HAPPY TO REPORT THAT THE NORMAL BLACK BUN MIX WORKS EXTREMELY WELL, REFASHIONED AS A TRAYBAKE. HERE'S HOW TO DO IT:

PREHEAT YOUR OVEN TO 190 DEG.

MAKE A SHORTBREAD MIX WITH 300G WHOLEMEAL PLAIN FLOUR, 200G BUTTER AND 100G SUGAR. YOU CAN DO THIS EASILY IN A FOOD PROCESSOR — BLITZ IT TILL IT STARTS CLINGING TO ITSELF IN A DOUGH-LIKE MANNER. PUT HALF OF IT IN A LINED TRAY (MINE IS 11 X 6 X 2 INCHES DEEP) AND PRESS IT ALL DOWN REALLY FIRMLY SO THAT YOU HAVE A NICE EVEN BASE. PUT IT IN THE OVEN FOR ABOUT 20 MINS.

MIX UP 300G CURRANTS AND 150G RAISINS, 50G DARK MUSCOVADO SUGAR, A TABLESPOON OF BLACK TREACLE, A TSP EACH OF MIXED SPICE AND GROUND GINGER, ½ TSP BICARB OF SODA, 1 TBSP OF WHISKY, AND AN EGG. GIVE IT A RIGHT GOOD GRINDING WITH THE BLACK PEPPER MILL. STIR IT ALL TOGETHER.

POUR YOUR 'FLIES' ONTO THE SHORTBREAD BASE AND LEVEL THEM OUT. YOUR CEMETERY SHOULD BE ABOUT ¾ INCH DEEP AT THIS POINT. SPRINKLE ON THE REST OF YOUR SHORTBREAD MIX, PRESSING IT DOWN QUITE FIRMLY. YOU WON'T BE ABLE TO MAKE IT AS FIRM AS THE BASE, BUT THAT'S OKAY BECAUSE YOU END UP WITH A NICE STREUSEL TYPE OF TOPPING — A LITTLE CRUMBLY — WHICH IS VERY ATTRACTIVE AND NEEDS NO FURTHER ADORNMENT.

BAKE FOR 45–50 MINS AT 180 DEG UNTIL IT IS NICE AND GOLDEN, WITH A WELL-COOKED LOWER CRUST. IT WILL SMELL FRAGRANT AND WELCOMING. CUT IT INTO SQUARES OR FINGERS; IT'S QUITE SUBSTAN-

TIAL. HAVE A DRAM OF THE SAME WHISKY THAT WENT INTO IT ALONG-SIDE; OR A CUP OF TEA IF THAT'S YOUR THING.

AFTER A COUPLE OF DAYS OF EATING THIS MORE OR LESS ON MY OWN (BLISS BUT FATTENING), I TOOK IT TO WORK AT THE DISTILLERY, AND IT WAS SCOFFED IN A MATTER OF MINUTES. DISTILLERY WORKERS HAVE A PRACTICAL SENSE OF TRADITION, SO THE IDEA OF A BLACK BUN THAT COULD BE MADE MUCH MORE CONVENIENTLY THAN THE ORIGINAL APPEALED GREATLY. THEY WANTED TO KNOW WHAT WAS IN IT, AND WHAT KIND OF WHISKY. NOT THAT IT MATTERS; BUT I WOULDN'T USE A FINE MALT FOR SUCH A RECIPE. I HAD SOME GROUSE IN THE BACK OF THE CUPBOARD, AND IT DID THE JOB VERY NICELY.

CHAPTER 11: FRIENDS AS FAMILY

Harry got fixated on a career as an army officer. His father and I weren't exactly happy about it, having spent our youths clad in duffle coats adorned with CND badges. I will allow that I may have been underinformed about all things military. When I asked Harry why he wanted to waste his brains and youth in the service of a murderous regime, he raised his eyebrows in that really irritating 14-year-old way: 'Oh for goodness sake Mum, you must surely know that 90% of all peacekeeping is done by countries' armed forces?' Oh yeah?

For the sake of peacekeeping I decided to support him in his application process – after all, it wasn't as if he was proposing a life of drug addiction and violent crime, was it? Well, maybe the latter. Some parents would have seen it as a perfectly respectable career aspiration. But Bernard couldn't do it; he remained opposed and couldn't suspend disbelief. Harry wanted to apply for a place in a defence-sponsored sixth-form college down in England, which would prepare and sponsor students through an engineering or science degree, and then onto officer training in one of the three armed forces (army, navy, air force) or the Ministry of Defence. This would involve him leaving home at the age of fifteen and a half, to enter boarding school. My blood ran cold at the thought. Fifteen and a half? Boarding school! But Harry was full of joy at the prospect – a life of adventure, travel, new friends, and freedom from parental restrictions. I remembered that feeling from my own teens. Bernard was appalled. 'Look,' I said, 'we can't just forbid him to do this. It would really alienate him. He'd hate us forever. In any case – he won't be accepted.'

'Whyever not? He's a bright kid with loads of potential. They should be honoured.'

'Yes I know, but he's not one of them. They'll be looking for kids from military families, with posh backgrounds. Or else they'll be looking for English kids who live nearer by. Or kids with English qualifications rather than Scottish. If we let him apply and he gets turned down, we'll have to comfort him but at least we won't get the blame for ruining his life.'

Bernard still couldn't face it, so I said I'd do the ferrying backwards and forwards to interviews, if required, and help Harry fill in the forms. Anyway, long story short, the wee Wunderkind charmed the interview panels all the way through the lengthy selection process, and got a letter saying he was accepted, so long as he passed his Standard Grades at B or above. When his exam results came, he was off up north with a few friends, camping, and had agreed I should open his envelope, phone him, and read him out the results. Lump in my throat, I did so. He was on the beach at Findhorn on the Moray Firth. When I told him he had straight As, he dropped the phone to go cartwheeling across the sands. Jubilant. I was so pleased for his success, and so cut up about him leaving home, so soon. But, hey. That's what parenting is for, isn't it? I tried to see this as a success for him and for us too, but it was difficult.

Off he went to the military school, still proclaiming himself a vegetarian and thereby sentencing himself to two years of macaroni cheese (I'm not exaggerating entirely. They weren't imaginative about vegetarian options). At home, he'd settled on a 'no red meat' policy which suited us all quite easily, but he found this wasn't easily understood by the army school kitchens; and I guess he was sending me a message about being free to make his own decisions. Anyway, I stressed a little about his diet but otherwise could see he was being well looked after, getting an excellent education with lots of extra opportunities which we wouldn't have been able to provide, performing well in everything, bringing home great reports, and generally having the time of his life. He was pulling away from home, growing up, being himself, and I just had to accept it.

Boarding school had absolutely no place in our family history. As we saw it, it was for posh kids. We felt like fish out of water; although as it turned out, there was a fairly wide social mix at the school, with all places being subsidised to an extent. Still it felt strange, sewing on thousands of nametapes to every last bit of kit (nametapes on socks? Weird). The whole experience felt like Hogwarts; JK Rowling's first book ('Harry Potter and the Philosopher's Stone') had come out when my Harry was about eight; I read him the first chapter one bedtime and he took it off me and read the whole of the rest of the book himself. It was a major influence on his early literacy skills. Hogwarts, the school for junior wizards, has moving staircases and portraits which gossip with each other; feasts that descend ready-made from the rafters of the banqueting hall; a magical game played on broomsticks where the capture of the golden snitch, a little golden orb with feathery wings, wins the day. In my childhood I'd read such racy stuff as 'Last Term at Malory Towers', and even then, boarding school seemed exciting. How could we compete with the dream of Hogwarts?

The year Harry went to military school, they had just moved into brand-new premises; but the interviews had been held in the old school, a ruined abbey a few miles further north/nearer home.

The abbey could have been used as a movie set for Harry Potter, but the new school had marvellous sporting and other facilities. We took him down with his suitcases of lovingly-labelled garments, and he could scarcely contain his excitement. We saw his room, met his room-mates, had a cup of tea, got shown round the grounds and the brand-new climbing wall, swimming pool, and all manner of fancy equipment. We had all too brief a hug, and I wept for the first hundred miles back north.

Without labouring the point, I found myself unhappy in the marriage with no child at the heart of it; and after some heart-searching and lots of unhappy discussions, Bernard and I separated soon after my 50th birthday, during Harry's final year at school.

Way back in the day, I'd seen myself having a big family – six children, I thought, would be just lovely – but of course I'd had the miscarriages and, finances not being endless, we'd probably never have coped financially. I'd been lucky to get such a great kid and eventually accepted that we were a one-child family. But I'd always wanted to cook for more – and indeed that's what I'd done, all through the years – we always had big sizzling dishes of home-made whatever in the middle of the table, with second helpings the norm, and leftovers for the next day, or the freezer, or chance visitors. I loved it; it was part of who I was. Suddenly, living on my own, I had no-one to cook for.

This is just a practical expression of feeling lonely. I felt intensely alone in the world. With both my parents long gone and my brother and sister at a distance, and no other extended family, I had moments of true panic. I'd had occasional anxiety experiences throughout my life, but I always found solace in getting the pots and pans out. Soon after moving into my own place I had a night out with my friend Rhona and her sister Sheila; and late into the night tried to express my sense of loss in terms of not having anyone to feed. 'Just get six drunken women round the table,' said Sheila, who, some years previously, had been through the divorce/children leaving home experience. 'You don't need family if you've got good friends.'

These were wise words. I was shy about inviting people to come to tea/supper/dinner with me, always imagining that they had their own families to be with, or their own preferred routines. Especially people who were part of couples. But I started anyway, inviting friends home, and it was a real joy from the start. To my surprise, I discovered that the world was full of single, divorced or widowed people who enjoyed company as much as I did. I also realised that not everybody could cook. Or else they knew how but they'd lost interest, or forgotten how, or didn't have time. Most of my friends had travelled a lot and liked good food, so they were delighted to come to my table and have a delicious meal. Most of them liked eating out, and so did I, but I couldn't afford it very often. It worked well all round.

I especially remember one Easter, maybe the first after the end of my marriage. Easter was important to me. Back then, I had a regular churchgoing habit, and I liked all the culinary traditions that went with different aspects of the church year. Easter is a time of major celebration for Christians, so I didn't want to spend it alone. But I felt that it was a family time, and I didn't want to intrude on other people's plans. I looked around at those friends of mine who also followed some kind of religious observance, and recognised that some of them would also be alone for various reasons. Although they didn't all know each other, I decided to invite Joanne, Derek and Hilary to Easter Sunday lunch around my tiny kitchen table.

I can't remember what we ate. I'm sure I would have wanted to cook lamb, for tradition, but Joanne is/was a vegetarian so it must have been something else. What I do remember is that a few tears were shed for recently departed doggy friends (I thought I should get the obvious challenges out of the way at the start. So my introduction of Hilary and Joanne started with 'one of the things you have in common is that both your dogs died recently.' Okay, I'm not always the most tactful woman on the planet.) Having got that over with, and raised a glass to the memories of Monti and Max, we all got pleasantly bonded and had a brilliant afternoon together, with Derek acting as butler and squeezing out from behind the table so that he could get into the fridge for more wine, or whatever else I needed passing as the meal went on. I was so happy. It was just like having family around me. I'd found a way of negotiating the perils of midlife singlehood.

HOW AN ARMY MARCHES ON ITS BELLY

Several years later, during Harry's training at Sandhurst, he and all his fellow cadets ate 6,000 calories a day. Or was it 7,000? Loads, in any case. This was to enable these youngsters to survive sleep deprivation, running over the mountains with 400lb backpacks, crawling along ditches on their bellies to surprise the enemy, and learning how to kill a sack-and-sawdust body with a bayonet. It was unimaginably tough and I'm sure I don't know the half of it. So how do you manage all those calories (not that I recommend trying, if you're in a less active job)?

Double helpings. Maybe double-double. At the double.

Soups, stews, pies, tatties, doughballs, pizza, fish and chips, bread in all its forms, hot and cold puddings. Beer?

Fruit and veg to ward off scurvy and ease the way of all that stodge through the digestive system.

Fortunately by this time, Harry had given up his commitment to vegetarianism. I can't imagine how you would ramp up the necessary calories without meat, and without putting on loads of weight. I daresay some of the cadets must have

108

MANAGED IT BUT YOU WOULD HAVE TO BE VERY DISCIPLINED IN YOUR FOOD CHOICES. NOT THAT THEY WERE DOING THE COOKING OF COURSE. AS YOU MAY REMEMBER, MY MOTHER HAD BEEN A COOK IN A NAAFI CANTEEN DURING THE WAR, AND I HAD NO ILLUSIONS ABOUT THE QUALITY OF THE CUISINE MY WEE BOURGETTE AND MINACH-TRAINED LADDIE WOULD BE ENJOYING. GELATO DI FRAGOLA? HA! THAT'LL BE THE DAY!

WHEN THEY WERE OUT ON 'EXERCISES', THEY WERE ISSUED WITH 'RAT PACKS', MEANING 'RATION PACKS'. LITTLE BOIL-IN-THE-BAG MEALS THAT YOU COOKED IN MESS TINS WHICH TOOK UP THE MINIMUM SPACE IN YOUR BACKPACK, AND (ALLEGEDLY) CONTAINED ALL YOU NEEDED FOR GOOD NUTRITION. SOME OF IT, I BELIEVE, HAD TO BE REHYDRATED AND THEN HEATED OVER A FLAME. LIKE THOSE AWFUL SCI-FI SCENARIOS WHICH PROPOSE EATING PILLS INSTEAD OF FOOD.

NEEDLESS TO SAY, HE SURVIVED — A MASSIVE ACHIEVEMENT, AND I WAS IMMENSELY PROUD OF HIM AT HIS PASSING-OUT PARADE. I STILL AM. AND MY OPINION OF THE ARMY HAS CHANGED SOMEWHAT. THEY GO THROUGH SUCH PRIVATIONS TO KEEP US SAFE — IGNORING THE POLITICS AND THE FOLLY AND ALL THE REST OF IT. I SALUTE THEM. IF I HAVE A SECOND INCARNATION I WOULDN'T MIND TRAINING AS AN ARMY COOK — KEEPING OTHER WOMEN'S CHILDREN NOURISHED. AND DESPITE IT ALL, STRIVING FOR PEACE.

CHAPTER 12: ZANZIBAR!

I'm a little nervous; not sure if I'll be welcomed, so different I feel. I've decided to attend the main service at the Episcopal Cathedral in Stonetown, even though it's in Swahili. There are slave sculptures in the grounds, marking the struggle for emancipation; I'm hoping for a sense of connection with 'real' Zanzibaris.

The population here is 90% Muslim; I'm disconcerted when men call out to me in the street ('Hello Mama!') while the women scurry away indoors. The five-a-day call to prayer has a sweet kind of eeriness to my western ears; maybe going to church will help me find a balance. I'm given a hymn book and welcomed with a smile; this could be home. I walk into the massive cathedral, already nearly full; seeking a quiet corner. It looks like mine is the only white face. I slide along a pew near the back at the right, and a youngish man smiles and makes space. 'Welcome,' he says, and I thank him. Then he tells me that the priest always welcomes new people too – publicly. I will be asked to introduce myself. Help! The young man says he will signal when I have to stand up and do the business. I can just about do it in Swahili, I remind myself, hands sweating.

The service begins and everyone is on their feet – maybe 500 people? The familiar murmured responses calm me a little. Then the singing begins.

There is a swell; it feels like I'm on a catamaran out on the Indian Ocean, the waves slapping me this way and that, up and further up, and ever further from the shore. Those voices! Intermingling harmonies, stray high notes, bottom-bangers. It's breathtaking.

The priest calls visitors to identify themselves, and my neighbour gives me the nod. I stand, biting my lip. The priest goes round everyone and being so close to the back, I'm last. I stammer out a line which I hope informs them that my name is Helen and I come from Scotland; then sink down with relief. My neighbour smiles at me. The girl done good.

A choir lines up out front and belts out a few energetic numbers, great theatre.

Then the next hymn is announced; I know the tune; it's 'Oh Jesus I have promised,' and I can mouth the Swahili words and join in; maybe even adding an alto line. This is joyful. I'm beginning to feel at home. The voices around me are rousing and plangent; how thrilling to be surrounded by so many male voices. I glance around. Men everywhere. To my right, to my left. Before me and behind. Where are all the women? A little niggle enters my brain and I crane to look over to the other side of the church. Ah. There they are, with the children; a whole phalanx of women, colourful and relaxed, singing lustily, filling the pews all down the left-hand side of the cathedral. Separate from the men.

What a gaffe.

ALL MY LIFE I'd been aware of world hunger. Starving children in Biafra filled the television screens when I was around 12, and my mother's determined justification for Cabbage Wars was that other children less fortunate would be grateful (therefore so should I). At school, I learned in geography about climatic zones and the impact of temperature, flood, and drought. After school I learned about history and politics. Then of course all the standard and worthy charitable activity was updated and made hip by Bob Geldof in 1984 – Feed the World; Do They Know It's Christmas? I got involved in various church-based activities to raise funds for overseas projects. So I had no illusions that my daily bread was enjoyed in similar measure across the planet. I thought it would be a fine thing to go and live abroad for a while and do some voluntary work – something 'really worthwhile'; but this was a remote kind of dream-plan and I couldn't quite see the way forward to make this happen.

In my fifties, divorced and living alone and having to be very careful with my finances, I found that work was harder to come by than heretofore. A research job which I was loving was suddenly whipped from under me – it had been a two-year contract, but I'd been given reason to expect it to continue. This left me floundering a little. For the first time in my life I wasn't getting every job I went after; I'd go along to interviews feeling well prepared and knowing I had a lot to offer, only to find myself competing with youngsters in suits. And they were the ones who got the jobs. I took on a series of temporary contracts in jobs which were okay, but not as fulfilling as they might be. Someone in my poetry group asked me why I didn't just rent out my house and go and do voluntary work overseas – surely, she reasoned, I had nothing to lose? So I looked into it, did the sums, started following the trail, and eventually found myself accepted, trained-up, and ready for the off. We were approved in principle, and then had to wait for specific projects to come up which were felt to match our skillsets. I have always had a tendency to think I can do anything if I only try. Ah, hindsight!

My first offer was Zanzibar, and I seized at it greedily. Zanzibar! The photos made it look like an advert for Bounty Bars to which

I had always been partial. (Only the plain chocolate ones.) Well it wasn't just about the Bounty Bars, it was general impatience. I felt as if my life was absolutely stuck – work I didn't enjoy, no good relationships with anyone who might become a new partner in life, and my Pride and Joy far away at University, planning his eventual army career, and never likely to come home properly. And 2009–10 was a helluva winter, with record snowfalls. So off I went. What did I have to lose? As I boarded my connecting flight from Edinburgh to London I was given a free copy of 'The Scotsman', with a complimentary section of photos sent in by readers all around snowy Scotland. I browsed through it en route for Dar es Salaam and laughed: hah! No more snow for me!

After three weeks' training on the mainland (Swahili language and culture), I and five other new volunteers were sent across on the two-and-a-half-hour ferry to Zanzibar, to contribute to various projects already underway. My 'employer' was a sort of community development organisation, the charitable wing of a wealthy airline and hospitality organisation; and it proved difficult to clarify exactly what their expectations were. They provided me with housing and a small volunteers' allowance; however on Day One, fresh off the ferry, they sent me alone to the market to buy a kerosene stove, and a gallon of kerosene plus basic food supplies, because there was a power cut. I found it pretty overwhelming.

We'd heard about the power cut while still on the mainland and I hadn't been concerned; I imagined it would be well and truly over by the time we got there. In my experience, power cuts lasted up to 12 hours but only in extreme circumstances. Sometimes the electricity was back on before you had found the matches to light the candles. But not in Zanzibar. In total, the power cut lasted three months, although we arrived two-thirds of the way through, so 'only' had one month to contend with. It was horrific! Zanzibar, at 7 degrees south of the equator, was extremely hot and humid at the best of times. Without electricity there was no air conditioning, the electric fans didn't work, there was no refrigeration, no cooking facilities, no light, no pumps so the toilets wouldn't flush after the tanks emptied. You can imagine the scale of the challenge.

Hygiene was really tricky. We'd all had a full range of vaccinations before leaving home, and had to take ongoing anti-malarial treatment – antibiotics usually, as these were the cheapest if not the most effective. The water supply was unsafe, and we always had to filter then boil any water we used, even for brushing teeth. Insects were everywhere, and not having a fridge meant food could barely be kept for a day. Ants used to get into the bread. Just making the most basic of meals involved careful planning. And daylight arrived at 7am, departed at 7pm – so you couldn't linger outside. You think candlelight is romantic? Try cooking your dinner on your kerosene stove, at floor level among the cockroaches, by candlelight. Danger abounds.

For the first week I was living alone in a house about 30 minutes' journey from the town centre. The 15-seater minibus – or *daladala* – never left the terminal until there were at least 20 people jammed in. I would emerge sweaty and stressed with a 20-minute walk at dusk, through potholes, to get back to an empty house. Not quite empty – a guard had been appointed, a young man of 18 named Mohammed whose English was even more rudimentary than my Swahili. He would arrive about five minutes after dark, sleep on the verandah, and depart with first light. The house I'd been given was quite big, in a concretey and tinny sort of way, and set inside a locked compound. Then there were more locks to get onto the grilled verandah, and a further set of locks to get in through the front door. When the birds landed on the roof in the middle of the night it sounded like footsteps shuffling up the hallway towards your bedroom. Trapped in there, sweating under my mosquito net, I would lie awake terrified, and reminding myself how many barriers an intruder would have to breach to gain entry; it took a major effort of reason to stay calm.

After a week another volunteer arrived to share the house, and in some ways that was a relief; however she wasn't easy to get on with. Minnie was a 30-year-old Ugandan woman, with very firm religious/cultural beliefs, which she assumed I would share. Right at the start (because of the birds on the roof), she formed a belief that our house was haunted, and therefore must have been cursed – probably, she thought, by an old woman who lived opposite. A thin, anxious old lady had rattled at our compound railings on my first day and asked for a cleaning job. I'd looked up my Swahili phrasebook and said no thank you, as I knew we couldn't afford a cleaner. That, Minnie thought, would be reason enough for her to curse us. 'You know what old women are like,' she said. Well, what could I say? I was already over 20 years older than Minnie, so she probably saw me as on that dangerous journey.

So Minnie, a firm Christian believer, set out a system of prayers and hymns which, she assured me, would banish the evil spirits. There are sections of the Psalms which I had never taken seriously, believing firmly that, if She is anything, 'God is love.' In these psalms, King David (the writer) invokes God's wrath on the miscreants who are making his life misery. Just up Minnie's street. She intoned the prayers ('Smite the bastards!' or words to that effect) and ordered me to sing the hymns. I was still trying to demonstrate my willingness to see the world from a non-colonial perspective and faced with her demands, I couldn't think of anything else to do but comply. It would soon be over and then I could escape to my own room, mosquito net, candle and book. Phew. But then on her second night she wanted to do it all over again! I rebelled on the fourth night, to her utter bewilderment and annoyance, and after that we never quite managed to cultivate a cosy housemate ambience.

Inner conflict reigned. I knew other cultures would have different expectations and no one religious group had the absolute truth on how things should be. I thought I was ready to be flexible and non-judgemental and open to new experiences. But I couldn't sit there and listen to prayers for an old woman to be exorcised of imaginary evils. And then Minnie (a native Swahili speaker) made some arrangement for a cleaner which I couldn't understand, requiring me to pay half the wages but then instructing the cleaner to do all Minnie's personal laundry and clean her shoes rather than mop the kitchen floor; I lost it. Unexpectedly, and unlike me, it seemed that Minnie had grown up accustomed to having servants, and had no qualms about giving orders and settling terms which I saw as harsh. Our cultural divides were just too complicated, and left me with no space to find a comfortable way to be myself in a different world.

I eventually moved out, into a smaller and noisier flat in the centre of Stonetown, but on my own thank goodness, without a guard, and only a ten-minute walk from work. I'd started writing my first blog, and was now able to settle down quietly and pour my confusions and anxieties into my writing.

Zanzibar had been a major slave trading port in the 19th century, run by Arab traders and drawing slaves from all over East Africa. The Anglican cathedral in Stonetown is built on the foundations of the old slave market, the bishop at the time of the construction having wished to identify with the poor and oppressed, to make his own stand against slavery. David Livingstone, the 19th-century Scottish explorer and missionary, stayed in Stonetown and was part of the early battle to end the East African slave trade. There is a large sculpture in the cathedral grounds in the form of a slave pit, with five slaves standing waiting to go to market. You look down into it; the sculptured humans were carved out in the 1960s by a Swedish artist, but the chains that bind them are original chains used to imprison real slaves. It's very chilling.

Does the legacy of slavery live on in present-day Zanzibar? It was impossible for me as a short-term visitor to have any informed opinion. Since independence, Tanzania, and therefore Zanzibar, were run as a socialist state. Comparison is often made with Kenya, the country immediately to the north, which was ruled after independence with a more capitalist approach. And Kenya is much more successful in terms of business, farming and exporting. At least that's what I was told, by a Kenyan. Seemingly the hotels in Zanzibar were all run by the state until only ten years previously; entrepreneurialism was not embedded at the time of my stay. The markets were flooded with Chinese goods – beds, mattresses, textiles, domestic equipment. There was little sense of an indigenous culture. And women's opportunities were much more restricted than men's.

One of my colleagues at my placement agency, a young Arab man in his late 20s, commented that the thing I had which he did not was freedom. He was not free, he said, despite being quite successful educationally, to travel or to start a business or to do any of the things which he felt would improve his lot in life. (What he *was* free to do, should he choose, was to take a second or even a third wife. Polygamy was firmly enshrined for those who could afford it – not, of course, as a mutual thing whereby a woman could take a second husband.)

In this context, settling in was quite a challenge. I felt that people didn't trust me. Muggings and housebreakings were not uncommon. I felt very keenly the misperception that because I was white, I would be wealthy. And because I was a woman travelling alone, I was fair game.

Of course one of my chief preoccupations – feeding myself – was a whole new journey. The market in Stonetown comprised an old and permanent ramshackle of stalls, shaded by roofs but open at the side, and extensive. It was open every day apart from midday on Fridays, when the shops and stalls all closed for the men to go to prayers. At other times, men of all ages could be seen pulling two-wheeled bogeys loaded with long poles of sugar cane, all along the bus routes into town. Other goods such as mangoes and bananas, live chickens, meat carcases, were hauled in by ox-drawn carts – skinny beasts with humps on their necks to support the yoke. Which came first, I wondered: the hump or the yoke?

The market men always seemed a bit suspicious of me; or maybe I'd become paranoid. Some of the local people at work assured me that whenever a white face came by, the prices doubled. It was assumed that if you were white, you had plenty money – which of course I didn't. Volunteer allowances were fixed at 35,000 Tanzanian shillings (equivalent to about £35) a month which was apparently the average local wage. But the average local worker had an infrastructure and a large family around them; whereas I found I had to eke my shillings out. When I tried to buy just a couple of bananas in the market, the stall-holder wouldn't let me – he insisted I had to buy the whole hand (about 16 bananas), which was actually very cheap, so he couldn't understand why I only wanted two. But I knew that the other bananas would just go to waste. And attract flies. And in the meantime I'd have to lug them all home on the *daladala*, squashed in between the other passengers. So I declined, but felt frustrated. A banana would have made an easy supper for me; but it wasn't to be. It took me a couple of weeks to find bread for sale – little white loaves of about half a pound each, rather than chapattis – I guess they're not a traditional part of the Zanzibari diet, and in truth they were pretty insubstantial. But I found comfort in their relative familiarity so I got into a habit of buying one every day, and split it between supper and next day's break-fast – balancing it overnight on a plate at the top of a wide-necked bottle, to defeat the ants.

Dairy foods were very hard to find. Eventually I found a store that sold a tart, plain, natural yoghurt which was sublime; cheese was very occasionally available as a sort of rubbery Cheddar type, and felt like gold dust. Butter was unknown; they had 'Blue Band' margarine, which I hadn't seen back home since the seventies. Milk was hard to come by, but I could live without it. Eggs, though small, were plentiful. As you cracked an egg open you could tell its mother hadn't been a well-fed hen. Meat was cheap but the stalls were covered with flies. Vegetables were plentiful. Rice and chapattis were everywhere. Cooking for one was a challenge when refrigeration was unavailable.

There was a cheap and cheerful workers' café in town which the volunteers regularly used, where for a few hundred shillings (by today's exchange rates, 500 Tanzanian shillings is equivalent to 20p in British money) you could get a bowl of rice and a large ladleful of stew. The choice was always beef, chicken, vegetable, or octopus. Eating here was probably just as cheap as cooking for one, and much cheerier, so long as you could get home before dark. And I got the chance to eat octopus, which was interesting. Its warty skin detracted somewhat from the presentation, but the texture was less rubbery on the tongue than you'd expect, and I rather enjoyed it. I couldn't cultivate a taste for ugali – a sort of mealy paste made from sorghum which had the texture of play-dough. You kneaded it with the fingers of your right hand (never using your left hand for eating), to make a casing round whatever else was on your plate – a bit of octopus tentacle, for example – and popped it in your mouth. It was tasteless. I reasoned with myself that it was a bit like polenta, which I had enjoyed so much in Italy; but then polenta had a nice corny flavour while this was just bland stodge.

We'd been warned against eating fresh fruit because of the hygiene problem. When we arrived on the island in February it was mango season, and they looked and smelled fabulous – fragrant and a little spicy. By the beginning of March I was ignoring the dietary warnings and purchased some freshly prepared mango every day at a stall on my way back to the *daladala* terminus from work. The vendor would offer a little dark red powder as garnish and when asked what it was, he managed to communicate to me that it was a mixture of salt and chilli. Absolutely delicious! The other thing I ignored advice about was the freshly-squeezed sugar cane – the vendors pushed yard-long stalks of it through a mobile mangle, along with some halved limes, into a battered jug. They then poured you a plastic cupful and it tasted wonderful.

Fresh meat was a puzzle; I never saw animals being driven in on foot, or delivered by any other means. But once or twice a week, by 7.30am, there would be a steaming heap of cowskins, surrounded by bluebottles, right at the entrance to the market. Was there an actual abattoir, and what were the conditions? I suspect the cows were killed and butchered right there in the market, perhaps in an inner sanctum hidden from view, and probably in a Halal manner; but I'm just guessing. There were rows and rows of butchers' stalls under cover, in the middle of the market, with the more picturesque fruits and vegetables arranged round about. Nothing was refrigerated as far as I remember, and the cuts were unrecognisable to me. None of your neat hygienic cling-wrapped packages in Stonetown Market; it looked like chunks had been hacked off a skinny cow, with a view to feeding a large family for a fortnight. It was very intimidating. I stood and looked for a long time, debating whether or not to try to buy something; I was a dedicated traveller, or so I thought, ready to try anything. On my third visit I had a plan; I would try to buy some lamb, which would have to be smaller in size because sheep were smaller than cows. I had looked up the Swahili word for sheep but this didn't seem to mean anything to the vendors; maybe, like in English, the words 'mutton' and 'lamb' were different from the animal word? I put my fingers to my head like rams' horns and uttered a 'bah-aah-aah' sound and instantly they knew what I wanted; or at least they knew what they could sell me. I went home with a chunk of meat which Minnie informed me was goat. Never mind, I was ravenous and curious and had a project. I tried to fast-fry it for starters, to seal in the juices, but it was never easy getting the pot hot enough, so that failed. I added some water to the pot with a couple of onions, and left it simmering till the kerosene ran out. After I'd gone out for more kerosene and finished the job, I boiled some rice and invited my little group of fellow volunteers around. Tough, yes, but very tasty. We sat around like a bunch of cannibals, sucking the bones.

On another occasion I had invited the others and wanted to cook fish. But I couldn't find any. I trawled around some of the out-of-town markets, catching *daladalas* on unknown routes and finding the markets were all pretty much identical. At last I gave up and decided to cook a vegetable curry instead, and headed home with a heavy basket of yams and onions and tomatoes. I trawled up the road avoiding the puddles which took up most of the road (there had been monsoon-like rains for a few weeks). I was especially keen to avoid the spot where, the night before, I'd seen a drowned rat in among the detritus during a lull in the rain. Children just waded through the puddles and played on regardless, but I was spooked by the rat. Anyway, just as I arrived back at my triple-locked fortress, a man came along on a bike, selling fish. He had a rod on his shoulder, and it looked like this was his personal catch. I bought four little fish in dazzling sequinned costumes, all turquoise and azure and crimson. Gorgeous. Then I spent over an hour scraping their scales off and slipping their guts out. By the time I was ready to cook, the wee white fillets looked pretty ordinary. But hey, it's the journey that matters, not the destination!

Cathy, one of the other volunteers, had a birthday while I was still sharing the house with Minnie. I thought I'd have a go at making a birthday cake for her, having discovered a shop at the *daladala* stop which sold loose flour by the kilo. There were a number of challenges to overcome: no cake tin, no oven, no wooden spoon. Probably birthday cake was a mad choice of dish to try to make in those circumstances. I turned out a loose puddingy mixture onto four plates and we all devoured it like it was the finest offering from the Scottish artisan bakery Fisher & Donaldson.

A birthday cake – in Zanzibar? What on earth bound us all to such inappropriate traditions? I guess we were homesick. It wasn't easy making friends with local people – the men all wanted to practice their English on you as you passed by, and as you walked down the street you were assailed by constant cries of 'hey, Mamma! Hey, Sister!' and requests for your phone number. The women had usually left school earlier and had very little English, and were expected to stay inside; so there was little chance of getting to know any of them. Being white set up inevitable barriers; once I tried to help an old crippled man down some steps. He immediately shot out his hand, palm up, begging for money. In my street, hordes of children used to chase me chanting one of their few English phrases – 'give me money!' then scattering, giggling, as I shook my head in despair.

Although my job was very badly organised, there was one project which had a modicum of order and purpose to it. We had funding to set up an employability project for young Zanzibaris, to equip them for jobs in the hospitality and tourism industries. It was only ten years or so since tourism had gone commercial on the island – until then, there was one hotel in Stonetown, and it was state-owned. There had been a rash of hotel growth all over the island, mainly by international chains capitalising on the stunning scenery; and theoretically, plenty of jobs. But these mainly went to youngsters coming over from the mainland, or from neighbouring Kenya. It seemed that Muslim families had strong reservations about allowing their children to work in hotels; they were concerned about their daughters in house-keeping roles being confronted with half-dressed men as they went about their cleaning duties; or their sons working behind bars and handling alcohol. They watched white tourists strolling around Stonetown in shorts and skimpy tops, and concluded that this was not a world they wanted their youngsters to inhabit. Also, from the employers' point of view, it was said that local employees were less reliable than others – if there was a funeral, everyone downed tools and stayed off for at least a whole day, no matter how tenuous their connection with the deceased. Language was also a problem – not just for communicating with tourists, but also with supervisors and bosses from far away. Theoretically, children were taught English at school; but this was rudimentary. Only the lowest-paid jobs were available to those whose only language was Swahili. Many of the biggest and best hotels, away on the north coast, were Italian or German, and they wanted staff who could speak those languages. So it wasn't easy for the local kids. My own stumbling efforts with Swahili reminded me how hard it was to genuinely communicate in a language not your own.

So, a basic but somehow complicated three-month programme had been set up, to teach unemployed local youngsters the basics required for a job in the hospitality and tourism sector. I helped to run it, and gained a close-up view of the challenges faced by the young people. This included trying to teach via an interpreter. I was allocated 'equalities' as the subject of my lesson and this was so out of reach as to be ridiculous. In my past experience, 'equalities' included race, religion, age, gender, sexuality. Race, they understood already from their own life experience – what could I teach them? Religion was beyond questioning because it had provided the framework for their lives and they were not permitted to explore its potential traps. Age was relatively straightforward. Gender was easy for me to talk about but hard to challenge the everyday discrimination we all (as women) experienced. For them this included not being allowed to swim in their own beautiful ocean in case they 'incited' men to rape. Every day after school you could watch the young boys tearing down to the pier, casting off their clothes, and diving in with utter abandon. It was beautiful to watch their energy and sheer joy – until you looked behind you and saw a little group of girls clad all in black, sitting well away from the water's edge, whispering among themselves. What were they whispering about? They may have been planning their own liberation, for all I knew; but it didn't look like it was going to happen anytime soon. And then there was the question of discrimination on the grounds of sexuality – in a country where homosexual acts are punishable by lengthy prison sentences. I asked my colleague how I should teach sexuality inequality. 'Just leave it out,' he replied.

Other aspects of the course were equally frustrating. The basic kitchen skills part of the course was put on hold because the catering college was waiting for new kitchens to arrive. At the time of my involvement, these were stuck somewhere in Nairobi, but nobody was too concerned because they would be with us in eight weeks or so. Only eight weeks! In a three-month programme! Everyone who taught any aspect of the course was trying to assert their needs in order to do a proper job, but my organisation which was co-ordinating the whole process (and held the budget for it) just brought in extra layers of bureaucracy to sort things out. The students were supposed to have three months' teaching followed by a three-month placement, but these placements hadn't been set up and nobody seemed to be in a hurry to do it. Back home I had worked in sectors where students on placement were just seen as free labour, and I could see that this could easily happen here too. I discussed a placement agreement contract with my colleagues and they agreed, and said I could go round the hotels and meet with their HR people to try to set up good placements.

When, nowadays, I meet people who have holidayed in five-star hotels in Zanzibar, I am really glad to have been a volunteer. They swoon in enchantment; they gasp at the opportunities I had. Quite right, too. It was unique. And showed me the difference between being a tourist, and living in the local situation – even if I was only there for a short time and had a means of escape.

However I am also glad that, just towards the end of my time there, I got to see some of those top-end hotels. They really were beautiful – tranquil oases of cool and calm, gently framed by Arabic columns and arches; ceiling fans keeping the hot air circulating, and a waiter never far away to bring you something cool and refreshing. So I know what kind of experience those tourists have had, and it has no doubt been heavenly. I took a group of five of our best students to visit a hotel in Stonetown run by the Aga Khan hotel group. We were shown round by a female HR manager, a dignified lady about my own age dressed modestly and with her hair covered – no doubt she was Muslim. She was very firm with the students, telling them about the hotel's high expectations of staff. And she also told them about uniforms to be worn, the laundry arrangements, the staff facilities for showers, the meals provided. She corrected one of the girls who came too close to her in greeting, explaining people's need for personal space. She corrected one of the boys whose speech was too offhand, explaining that all staff represented the hotel in their behaviour. These were youngsters who had been unemployed for at least six months before coming on our programme; their experiences were limited and their hopes modest. Their faces, their eyes and mouths, their entire bodies lit up with hope. Just being shown round by a woman in a senior position was life-changing for them. Never mind those students – I too wanted a job in that serene, cool, well-organised hotel!

Other hotels, especially those on the north coast, were run by multinational companies and when I spoke to their HR managers on the phone, they were interested in our students but somewhat cynical. They had past experience of hiring local youngsters and being let down in various ways. Nearly none of the students I was seeking placements for were willing to live away from home, which would have been necessary for the north-end jobs; for even though Zanzibar was small – no bigger than the Isle of Arran, off the west coast of Scotland – the road network was primitive and it took six hours by *daladala* to get there from Stonetown.

One of my volunteer companions was carrying out some research on tourism, on behalf of an organisation which was campaigning for green, or sustainable, or ethical tourism. I learned that the multinationals' business practices took a lot and gave very little back to the local area – thereby feeding the general air of mistrust. A hotel might take up a whole stretch of beach which had previously provided an income in terms of fishing or seaweed-gathering for a whole village. Most of the hotel's supplies would be imported. Even 'local' food would come from the mainland, for the sake of reliable supply; much of it from abroad. And as I had already learned, there were very few jobs in those hotels for local people. I will probably never do voluntary work overseas again; and if ever I can afford to go back to Zanzibar I will definitely want to go to a nice hotel with good air conditioning and a private beach. However I now understand how to travel respectfully and how ethical tourism practices can make a difference in the world, and this was hard learning. Somehow, whatever the difficulties, you have to get into conversations with the people who are already there, and hear their perspective. You have to have respect for the locals; and if you're not ready to do that, you should stay at home.

FAILSAFE VEGGIE CURRY

I'M LUCKY TO BE GIVEN LOTS OF COURGETTES, CUCUMBERS AND LETTUCES EVERY YEAR BY KEEN GARDENING FRIENDS. OCCASIONALLY ALSO MARROWS AND CORIANDER. AND LOTS OF OTHER THINGS TOO, BUT THOSE ARE THE THINGS THAT APPEAR MOST OFTEN. SEEMINGLY, IF YOU'RE GREEN-FINGERED (WHICH I'M NOT), THESE ARE PROLIFIC CROPS. THERE ARE LOADS OF THINGS YOU CAN DO WITH GLUTS — SOUP IS THE OBVIOUS CANDIDATE, AS ARE VARIOUS CHUTNEYS AND RELISHES. BUT A GOOD VEGGIE CURRY, LIKE THE ONES THEY SERVE BY THE VAT IN ZANZIBAR, IS A GREAT THING TO BE ABLE TO RATTLE UP WITHOUT RECOURSE TO A RECIPE, ONCE YOU'VE MEMORISED A FEW POINTS:

1. USE YOUR VEG WHILE IT'S STILL NICE AND FRESH, GIVE IT A WASH AND TAKE CARE WHEN YOU'RE CHOPPING IT UP FOR THE POT. IT'S GOOD TO HAVE THE VARIOUS ELEMENTS OF A SIMILAR SIZE AND SHAPE.

2. FOR THE STORECUPBOARD:

A. KEEP A STORE OF CUMIN, CORIANDER AND CARDAMOM SEEDS ALONG WITH SOME DRIED CHILLIES. THEY'RE NOT EXPENSIVE AND THEY LAST FOR AGES (COMPARED WITH READY-GROUND, WHICH QUICKLY LOSE THEIR FLAVOUR).

B. GARLIC PASTE, IF YOU CAN'T BE BOTHERED PEELING AND CHOPPING THE FRESH BULBS.

C. OIL CAN BE RAPESEED, VEGETABLE, SUNFLOWER BUT NOT OLIVE — ITS FLAVOUR IS TOO PRONOUNCED AND COMES FROM THE WRONG PART OF THE WORLD FOR AUTHENTICITY, AND JUST DOESN'T 'GO'. IN ANY CASE, IT WOULD BE A WASTE OF A RELA-TIVELY EXPENSIVE INGREDIENT. YOU CAN ALSO USE COCONUT OIL, WHICH COMES IN A JAR AS IT SOLIDIFIES AT ROOM TEMPER-ATURE. THIS IS EXPENSIVE, BUT 'GOES'.

D. A TIN OF CHICKPEAS IS A HANDY ADDITION IF YOU NEED EXTRA BULK.

E. A TIN OF COCONUT MILK, EITHER FULL OR HALF-FAT, CAN BE USED INSTEAD OF WATER. OR A TIN OF TOMATOES.

F. LONG-GRAIN RICE. THERE'S QUITE A DIFFERENCE IN FLAVOUR BETWEEN THE CHEAPEST AND DEAREST, AND EVEN THE DEAREST GIVES GREAT VALUE. BROWN BASMATI IS MY FAVOURITE. THE EXTRA HUSK ON BROWN RICE GIVES A HUGE FIBRE BOOST TO YOUR DIET.

G. OPTIONAL EXTRAS FOR THE MIX, ALSO FROM THE STORE CUPBOARD — SESAME SEEDS AND RAISINS OR SULTANAS.

H. CHUTNEY OR PICKLE, YOUR OWN OR SHOP-BOUGHT. BRINJAL (AUBERGINE) CHUTNEY AND LIME PICKLE GIVE A REAL SHOT OF ACID, DEPTH, AND FLAVOUR WHICH ENHANCE YOUR CURRY BEAUTIFULLY. BUT THEY'RE NOT ESSENTIAL.

3. I ALWAYS START OFF WITH ONIONS — WHITE OR BROWN.

4. NATURAL YOGHURT MAKES A LOVELY ADDITION, ESPECIALLY IF YOU'VE OVERDONE THE CHILLIES, AND IF YOU HAVE A CUCUMBER YOU CAN GRATE IT, SQUEEZE IT DRY AND ADD TO THE YOGHURT WITH A LITTLE GARLIC AND SOME SALT FOR AN INSTANT RAITA.

5. FRESH CORIANDER IS ALSO GOOD TO SCATTER AT THE END. NOT ESSENTIAL, THOUGH.

TO MAKE THE CURRY:

- *FRY SOME SLICED ONIONS AND CHOPPED GARLIC IN OIL TILL THEY'RE SOFT AND GOLDEN, NOT LETTING THE GARLIC BURN (SO KEEP IT MOVING IN THE PAN).*
- *ADD A SPICE MIX OF CUMIN, CORIANDER AND CARDAMOM GROUND UP WITH SOME SALT, AND FRY FOR A FEW MINUTES.*
- *ADD CHOPPED-UP VEG AS AVAILABLE TO YOU. PUT THE HARDER ONES, WHICH TAKE LONGER TO COOK, IN FIRST – E.G. POTATOES, CARROTS – AND GIVE THEM 10 MINS ON THEIR OWN. THEN ADD THE REST OF THE VEG, ALL CHOPPED UP NICELY. GIVE IT A GOOD STIR, PUT THE LID ON, AND LET IT SWEAT FOR 5 MINUTES.*
- *ADD CHICKPEAS IF YOU WANT THEM.*
- *ADD LIQUID – THIS COULD BE WATER OR A TIN OF TOMATOES OR A TIN OF COCONUT MILK.*
- *TASTE AND DECIDE WHETHER IT COULD DO WITH A LITTLE SWEETNESS. IF SO, ADD A HANDFUL OF RAISINS OR SULTANAS.*
- *TASTE AGAIN AND DECIDE HOW MUCH CHILLI IT NEEDS TO SUIT YOUR TASTE – YOU WILL HAVE TO JUDGE THIS ACCORDING TO HOW STRONG YOUR CHILLIES ARE AND HOW HOT YOU LIKE YOUR CURRIES TO BE. BUT EVEN IF YOU LIKE IT HOT, DON'T BLAST THE FRAGRANT, SUBTLER SPICES YOU'VE ALREADY ADDED OUT OF RECOGNITION.*
- *GIVE IT A STIR, ADD A LITTLE MORE WATER IF YOU THINK IT NEEDS TO BE MORE LIQUID, TURN THE HEAT DOWN, PUT THE LID BACK ON AND LET IT SIMMER FOR ABOUT HALF AN HOUR.*

SERVE WITH BOILED RICE (DOUBLE THE VOLUME OF WATER TO RICE, COOKED IN WATER WITH SOME SALT AND A LID TILL THE WATER HAS ALL BEEN ABSORBED AND THE RICE IS COOKED); RAITA AS MENTIONED ABOVE, OR EVEN JUST PLAIN YOGHURT; AND CHUTNEYS.

(IN THE CAFÉ IN ZANZIBAR, THEY PUT COOKED RICE IN LITTLE OILED

TUBS. YOU COULD CHOOSE EITHER LARGE OR SMALL, AND THEY WOULD TURN THE TUB OUT ONTO YOUR PLATE ALONG WITH YOUR CHOSEN LADLE OF CURRY. THERE WOULD ALSO BE A LITTLE DISH OF CHOPPED CHILLIS ON THE TABLE TO ADD IF YOU WANTED MORE FIRE ON YOUR PLATE.)

TASTY, HEALTHY, CHEAP. AND THE LEFTOVERS ARE EVEN BETTER THE NEXT DAY. WHAT MORE DO YOU WANT?

CHAPTER 13: FRIDAY'S FISH – IS EVERYBODY HAPPY?

Finding good work didn't get any easier after my return from the tropics, and I found myself doing lots of part-time jobs of different types – some college teaching, tutoring for Higher English and lower level Maths, writing training materials – getting exhausted and spreading myself too thinly. I felt I needed to concentrate on one area, to consolidate skills and confidence, and of course to make a reasonable living. One of my jobs was different. I'd been recruited by my friend Sheila to a relief house-keeping role, which mainly involved cooking for a small group of older people, and although it was badly paid, I found myself really enjoying it – every other weekend, in among all my other jobs. The cooking seemed more real, and necessary, and creative, than some of the other jobs.

Unexpectedly, the full-time House Manager left, and I was asked whether I might apply for the job. The downside would be split shifts and poor wages, although meals would be provided. The upside would be the opportunity to develop my cooking skills, learn about menu planning and budgeting, and get some general discipline around my lifelong interest in food. I would have to do a Food Hygiene certificate, which was fine; and I'd be working with older people, which I'd always enjoyed. But the wages really were dire, and I'd have to give up my other freelance, better-paid activities. I consulted my friends; some said yea, some said nay. I decided to go for it.

My enthusiasm was high. I'd just read Clarissa Dickson Wright's memoir, 'Spilling the Beans', in which she tells the story of her high-life barrister career felled by trenchant alcoholism; and how she found redemption from the gutter by plying her exceptional cooking skills. I was neither an alcoholic nor an exceptional cook, but I shared her love of good food and storytelling.

My new job entailed cooking and managing the house for six ageing tenants; and we were run by a local management committee. I was well tuned to the issues faced in the ageing process and it was no bother to me at all to engage with my six tenants and keep an eye on their wider welfare. On the other hand, it took me a while to develop a bit of speed and efficiency in getting meals on the table on time, keeping the cleaning routines going systematically, and organising shopping deliveries. I worked Monday till Friday, from 8am till 1.30pm, then from 4 till 6pm, with other relief staff doing the weekend shifts. Fortunately the house was only five minutes' drive from home, so I could flake out between shifts. Do a washing and hang it up. Read a little. And invariably, have a wee siesta. It was hard going back to work at 4pm after my relaxed afternoon; but sadly non-negotiable. It could have been worse: the job had until recently entailed sleepovers, so that every night there was a member of staff present in the house. This arrangement had just changed, as staff costs had become too expensive with the introduction of workplace pensions for all staff and the new 'living wage', just a little higher than the legal minimum wage. Dropping the sleepover shift was an unpopular move with some of the residents. I wouldn't have taken the job if it was still sleep-in; so I had no issues with this aspect. However, in exchange I had to spend a lot of time checking the tenants' community alarm systems and dealing with the flak when the ancient fire-alarm system kept going off.

Because there were no staff on site round the clock, it was harder to cope with any wandering or confused behaviour (on behalf of the tenants, that is! My own wandering usually stayed in my own head). Officially, our organisation didn't deal with dementia, and any tenant who developed this sadly common condition would be required to move on to a more protected setting. But of course, when someone develops dementia there is always a slow gradual progress of the condition; and we all grew attached to each other, and tried to delay any drastic action, and compensate for shortcomings.

One winter late afternoon, we had a thunderstorm and the lights went off, just as I was arriving back for my second shift at 4pm. I phoned one of the committee members and she went to the chippie. I set the table by candlelight and boiled a kettle on the gas stove, and we all had a very cheery supper together while the electrician wrestled with our ancient wiring. Our one rather confused tenant, initially alarmed by the blackout, was calmed and cheered greatly by the candles; and started relating his memories of the wartime blackout, back home in Somerset with his mother and six sisters, nearly all of whom were now dead. Others joined in with their own memories. It was humbling for me to hear all this, and almost a disappointment when our lights came back on. That generation has such resilience, having lived through tremendous hardships and dangers, losses and disasters. In my own lifetime I have never had to queue for bread or go hungry. I've been lucky.

A Scottish Government report of 2006–7 had exposed shockingly poor nutrition in care homes, through lack of systems for monitoring calories in and out. If you couldn't lift your fork to your own lips, there was a 50% risk that nobody would notice. You could fade away to nothing before someone might wonder whether you were getting enough to eat, and by that time you might have suffered all kinds of side-effects of malnutrition. Further to this, successive surveys revealed a general picture of poor health issues in older people. Scotland's record is worse than for the rest of the UK. Is this a disgrace in a so-called advanced nation, or isn't it? Something to be proud of when we're trumpeting about our magnificent salmon and venison and scallops and beef and lamb and raspberries? I was horrified by this, and somewhat zealous that my six tenants would enjoy a good healthy diet.

As always, I cooked everything from scratch, and eschewed ready-made anything. I found to my (ill-concealed) disgust that the relief staff relied heavily on certain items like gravy granules and frozen Yorkshire puddings. I refused to buy these, but every time I went on annual leave, when the office manager was responsible for the shopping, I would come back to a cupboardful of what I termed junk. This irritated me no end, but I realised I wasn't going to win that one. I decided it wouldn't do the tenants too much harm on an occasional basis, so long as they got their fresh home cooking from me the rest of the time. Perhaps I was overly pedantic; some of the tenants weren't crazy about their greens, liked their chemical gravy well enough, and loved their cakes and biscuits. I decided there was nothing to stop them buying in their own sweeties and other treats, and was unshakeable. Not that I was entirely fascist – I did bake – as per my job description – I just tried to keep a bit of a balance. And everyone has a different idea of balance.

The committee's treasurer at that time, due to retire soon after I was appointed, was coy about telling me what my budget was for food purchase; I suggested that if I could see a spreadsheet showing different items, I'd be better able to shop effectively. He just ignored me – to my great annoyance. He was a retired accountant and obviously had lived out his entire career in a context where junior staff just did as they were told and didn't question things. I found this attitude completely unhelpful so I just bought, carefully, what I needed, and asked him every so often if I was operating within budget. I never got a straight answer yet. I figured out that actually, for £4.50 per person per day, I was providing three good meals to a high standard for my tenants, and spending either the same as, or somewhat less than, my predecessor; so I stopped worrying about it. The bulk of the shopping was delivered by the supermarket each week and I changed this slightly, by shopping for meat at the local butcher's.

For the first time in my life, I had the chance to 'develop a relationship' with my local butcher, as all the food writers recommend. The difference in quality between his meat, and the supermarket equivalents, was striking. So much juicier and more tender. On the other hand, his range was often a bit limited; so occasionally I would buy the odd thing from the supermarket to supplement. I always left a nice piece of beef, lamb or pork, or a free-range chicken, for the weekend staff to prepare for Sunday lunch, and they enjoyed that after the scraggy hens and stringy beef they'd been used to rescuing in the past. It compensated them somewhat for the horror of having to make gravy or Yorkshire puddings from scratch! (Or, indeed, smuggling in a packet of Bisto in their apron pocket.)

I also widened the range of fruit and veg that featured on the menu, and kept it seasonal. Home baking was an explicit part of my job description, with Scottish palates being pretty well programmed to regular cake consumption. So, with three-times-a-week practice, I became adept at turning out a good scone and pancake, and various kinds of sponges, gingerbreads, fruit loaves, buns and traybakes. Actually, I'd always enjoyed baking so this was a real pleasure. Early on in the job, before the frustrations crept in, I remember standing one rainy morning in the spacious kitchen, the radio on, grating fragrant nutmeg into my gingerbread mix and thinking, 'I get *paid* for this?'

I experimented with sugar substitutes, settling on one called Xylitol, a tree bark derivative, which was several times sweeter than cane sugar. Its advantage over other sugar substitutes was that it weighed the same as standard sugar – so you could just use Xylitol instead of the other, without having to footer about with complicated proportions. Also, sugar in recipes adds bulk as well as sweetness, so if you tried to use those little saccharin tablets, for instance, the structure of your baking would suffer. The Xylitol was quite successful, and nobody really noticed the difference, which was all to the good. However, there was one potential side-effect to Xylitol which was something you really don't want much of in a sheltered housing establishment. Diarrhoea. I think I found this out in the small print before it became an issue – or perhaps, before it became such a significant issue that anyone felt the need to tell me about it. Thank goodness. From then on, I used 50% each of sugar and Xylitol. I suppose I should still be using it, but it's very expensive and I find other ways of controlling sugar in my personal life. Currently, I'm looking into Stevia.

I've never claimed any special skills in the kitchen, but I discovered there was something I could do which many far more experienced cooks couldn't – I could do seven perfect poached eggs, served on buttered toast, and get them to the table before the toast went cold. This was one of the favourite suppers.

The chief foodie event of the week as far as the tenants were concerned was the Friday visit of the Pittenweem fish van, from the East Neuk of Fife where the fishing fleet still goes out. For me, too, it was a delight – as with the butcher, the range was narrow but the quality magnificent. Margaret, the fish van lady, had been pounding the same beat for 32 years. She and her husband took turns at driving the van, and their son went out on the boat to catch the fish. It was a Friday when the result of the 2016 referendum about leaving or staying in the European Union came out, and to my horror it was a narrow margin for leaving. I asked Margaret what her family and friends in the fishing industry thought about this, and she muttered, 'twenty years too late.'

It was always breaded haddock, chips and peas on a Friday, and I in my naivete and enthusiasm thought they'd all enjoy a change; so one day I bought salmon fillets instead – pound for pound, the same price as haddock – and served them proudly with new potatoes, broccoli and a creamy parsley sauce. There was a deadly silence as I put the plates on the table, and I wondered what was wrong. The youngest tenant spoke up: 'you cannae beat a nice bit of haddock.' So I went back to haddock every Friday, but bought extra fish every second week to freeze for the following Tuesday, and varied it between salmon or smoked haddock, which I sometimes made into a fish pie. Occasionally I did kippers at teatime, for those who liked them. I alternated chips with new potatoes, and varied the inevitable frozen peas for other green veg. But they were sticklers for the fish and chips tradition. On one occasion, I ran out of tartare sauce – catastrophic carelessness! – and crossing my fingers, made one from scratch as I had mayo, yoghurt, capers, lemons and gherkins in the fridge. I thought it would be detected and found wanting but they all just scooped it onto the sides of their plates and ate it without comment. Sometimes the best compliment you might not receive was that something you'd lovingly put together tasted just like shop-bought.

One of the tenants had come to us relatively young, in his mid-70s, because he'd been widowed and had a range of health problems and found it all too much to cope with. I asked him what he'd cooked for himself when he had been home alone, and he described his favourite meal, which was Birds Eye boil-in-the-bag fish in parsley sauce. On one of my (lovingly prepared from scratch) fish-pie days, I put his plate down in front of him and he beamed in delight before scoffing the lot. 'Did you enjoy that?' I asked him as I cleared the plates. 'Enjoy it? It was nearly as good as Birds Eye!' he pronounced.

I haven't as yet mentioned my blog, which I started in the summer of 2013. I had of course blogged previously – when I was in Zanzibar in 2010 – so it wasn't my first attempt. Blogging from overseas was a great way of keeping in touch with people, and keeping them up to date, and most of all, reflecting on what was going on around you. But when I got back home, I felt I had nothing interesting enough to say. Eventually life got more than 'interesting'; and I decided blogging would be a creative way for me to keep sane.

I called my new blog 'A Drawerful of Porridge', a reference to the well-documented routine observed in Scottish farming life, where extra porridge from the morning pot would be poured into a drawer to cool, then cut into slices for the midday al fresco 'piece' – to you and me, lunch. I have to say I can think of nothing less appetising than a slice of cold porridge for my lunch. Except maybe cold ugali, as experienced in Zanzibar. However, the thriftiness of the practice appeals to me. And I felt the metaphor of a drawerful of porridge gave plenty scope for a wide range of posts, all about current daily life in Scotland. At first my posts were about cultural events, but soon I started writing about daily Scottish food and drink; and that's what the blog has become.

So, working as a house manager in a sheltered housing project gave lots of inspiration and photo opportunities. However, truth be told, the job had its downside. Although the menu planning was challenging, not much value was accorded to it – or that's how it felt to me. Nobody really wanted to hear me going on about it. So in my blog, I could wax lyrical about my sugar-reduction efforts and my campaign against chemical gravy granules, and know that out there, somebody was listening! The blog helped me hold on to my belief that cooking for older people was an important job, even though the wages were dreadful, the shifts exhausting, and the status somewhere below zero. I was self-conscious about being caught taking photos of plates of food; but it transpired that the previous house manager used to do the same and post them on Facebook. So, all was well, and the joy of writing about it all had a truly motivating effect.

There isn't much status in cooking. That's a sad fact. I've read lots of great books by people who have become celebrity chefs and they say the same – it's hard work all the way, without much reward except for your pride in your own work. In my case, the blue-and-white striped tabard that I wore seemed to render me invisible. Nobody had high expectations. I shouldn't have minded this, but actually it took me a while to get used to it. So I welcomed training opportunities, which early on included the mandatory Elementary Food Hygiene. My friend Sheila, who had got me into this job in the first place, suggested I should study Food Hygiene to Diploma level, because then I would be qualified to teach Elementary Food Hygiene to other people. This sounded like a good plan to me, so I looked into it and signed up.

First I had to do an Intermediate level award – this is the qualification that all butchers in Scotland must have; I passed this with a Merit even though I'd found it pretty tricky. All that microbiology was a challenge to me – questions with black and white answers weren't my strong point, given my past studies in literature, psychology and sociology, and languages. Anyway I soldiered on, with help from Christine my tutor, and butcher-counter conversations; and then I signed up for the Advanced Diploma. This was a distance-learning module, and I have to say, really quite turgid. I was paying for it myself as, quite understandably, my employers couldn't see the point of an Advanced Diploma in anything for their house managers. However, to my delight, the committee agreed to provide cover for one afternoon shift per week to allow me to study. So every Wednesday afternoon I finished at 1.30 and went home, had a power nap, then hit the library with my memory stick, textbook, giant jotter and pencil case. No need to return for the four-till-six stint! Deep joy. Two of the committee members were retired Environmental Health Officers, and they were interested in what I was doing and gave me lots of hints, and anecdotes about food hygiene disasters they had known. It kept me sane, and believing in myself as someone with half a functioning brain.

I had thought that teaching Elementary Food Hygiene might make a good retirement job for me, as my 60th birthday was forthcoming, when I would be able to cash in my Council pension and claim my bus pass. So I was carefully doing my sums to see whether I might manage to give up the day job. However, an extra dimension came into play, just about a year before the significant 60th birthday. I met Dave.

Reader, my entire outlook changed! I cashed in my Council pension as soon as I hit 60, put my house on the market, handed my notice in to the committee, and did my last shift at the end of November 2016. By 7pm that night I was lying on Dave's sofa with my cat Suzi on my lap and a glass of wine in my hand; the first of many suitcases lying unpacked on the floor beside me. Life suddenly felt very, very promising.

AN ALTERNATIVE FISHY LUNCH

BUY SOME SMOKED PEPPERED MACKEREL FILLETS. CHOP THEM UP A BIT AND MIX THEM WITH A SLICED RED ONION, SOME CHOPPED CUCUMBER AND APPLE, AND A CREAMY DRESSING OF NATURAL YOGHURT. GIVE IT A GOOD STIR. IF YOUR MACKEREL WASN'T PEPPERED TO START WITH, GRIND IT ON AT THIS STAGE. SERVE ON WHOLEMEAL PITTA, WITH SOME FRESH GREEN SALAD AND A NICE THICK WEDGE OF LEMON.

MACKEREL IS IN GOOD SUPPLY IN THE OCEANS, AND FULL OF OMEGA 3 PLUS A RANGE OF ESSENTIAL MINERALS AND VITAMINS. I MADE THIS AT A DEMO AT MAGGIE'S IN DUNDEE ONE NIGHT AND THEY INVITED ME BACK SO THEY MUST HAVE MEANT IT WHEN THEY SAID IT WAS DELICIOUS!

CHAPTER 14: ALL CHANGE

I was 59 when I met Dave; he was 69. One day I finished my morning shift at 1.30pm as usual, did a rapid brush of teeth and squirt of perfume, and dashed off to Townhill Loch, where we'd agreed to meet for a first 'date', i.e. without any other friends present. We were both, as we later discovered, a little anxious about being stood up. However all was well, and by the time we'd walked round the loch together and had a cup of hot chocolate, we were holding hands and arranging to meet again. Then I was off back to work, my heart racing, and he was heading north to Newburgh. Excitement! I knew from the first that this wasn't just a fleeting fancy, and the prospect of a lasting relationship had me in thrall.

How did I meet the lovely Dave? I was in the habit of visiting my friend Valerie in Newburgh. She'd moved there a couple of years previously and got involved with the church. When they started inviting her to take the service, she was both nervous and excited; so I offered to go along in support, cooking lunch in advance and taking it to her place. She invited another couple of friends – Ann and Amanda – so I was with three former nurses, always good for a laugh and a bit of hellbent reality. We enjoyed

Valerie's reflections – 'sermon' is a terrible word and quite inapplicable in her case – and then had a good old bonding over lunch and a gin or two.

One night I drove up to Newburgh to participate in a Taizé service Valerie had helped put together. Taizé services originated during the Second World War in the Burgundy area of France, where a community of Christian brothers set up an ecumenical movement for peace and justice, using meditation and simple chanting as the foundation of their worship. The movement spread, and the town of Taizé has become a prominent site for pilgrimage, with thousands of people, mainly youngsters, congregating each year to pray for peace. Simple songs with repetitive lyrics are sung to evoke a sense of calm purpose. Unusually in my experience of Taizé services, Valerie had some musicians accompanying, whom she'd met in the local pub. One of them was Dave, on guitar, and that's where I first met him – ironically, given his firm aetheist-agnostic stance. He had such a lovely way with the strings, and a gentle air about him, and such a nice long pair of legs … well, you get my drift. Justice and peace took on new meaning for me that night. The next time Valerie was having one of her post-church lunches she invited Dave to join us. His first response was to say no thank you, as he was a vegetarian and reckoned he was too much of a nuisance for people to have to entertain. Valerie assured him that I was great at cooking for vegetarians (!), indeed the whole meal would be vegetarian with perhaps a tiny meat option for the carnivores. So he agreed. In any case, he had to come and set up a charity-shop guitar for Valerie's daughter Olivia, so it all kind of fell into place. With a bit of prompting all round, Dave and I managed to get it together. Ann and Amanda came too, and also my gay friend Derek, which confused Dave somewhat; but Valerie later put him right. It was very jolly. After lunch we sat around singing, to Dave's accompaniment. I never sing alone in public, but somehow I cast caution to the winds and gave a long-drawn out version of Donovan's 'Universal Soldier'. As great songs go, I'm sure I murdered it; but Dave's face betrayed no angst. He sang a lovely song I hadn't heard before – 'Hermless' by Michael Marra – a poignant little story about someone who goes harmlessly about life without anybody ever noticing he's there.

Despite my nerves, I felt I was on strong ground, doing lunch; one of the things I made was couscous with Shakshouka, a spicy North African vegetable stew in which eggs are poached, and Dave complimented me generously. I found out he was a Dundonian, and that he could look across the Tay from Newburgh on a clear day, and see Cox's Stack, just a hundred yards from the place he was born.

After the meal, Dave invited Valerie and me to tea, promising to make his 'killer hummus'; so I thought I'd make him a nice loaf. I decided on a braided cheese-and-chutney-filled job, from James Morton's bread book. I didn't want Dave to think I was too keen – perish the thought – but somehow my loaf kept on rising and rising, and to my embarrassment, I nearly needed a forklift truck to get it into his flat. He liked it; and he liked me; and I liked him. So all was well. We commuted backwards and forwards between Newburgh and Dunfermline, where I was still doing my cooking shifts. 'How long have you been a vegetarian?' I asked innocently, one day early on – secretly hoping of course that it was a passing phase from which he would soon recover. 'Oh,' he replied nonchalantly, 'since 1973.' So that was that. No likelihood of change. Never mind, I liked vegetarian food too and felt I could adapt.

I did my sums, and figured out that by various means, I could cash in my little pension pot at 60 and retire on slim pickings. So I did, and moved 35 miles up the motorway to Newburgh. There was no point in asking Dave to come and live in Dunfermline; he'd made it clear how much he loved Newburgh. And I've always been a bit of a rolling stone, and even after 30 years in Dunfermline, didn't mind moving on again. It's only a 40 minute drive; I can keep up with old friends. And it is so lovely having a partner in life. And Newburgh is delightful.

However all these fresh starts are not without their challenges. The greatest of these, for me, was Dave's vegetarianism – or indeed, his antipathy to all things meat, born of his disgust on a visit to an abattoir in the 70s. I couldn't say I hadn't been warned. It's not that I don't love vegetarian food – I do, as in fact I love most food. But Dave is particularly pernickety and will, I hope, not mind me saying in print that it drove me nuts! After all the cabbage-and-sago training that my mother inflicted on me, I strongly value an ability – a willingness – a gratitude, even – to eat whatever is put in front of you, especially when half the world is starving. Also, the enjoyment of a shared meal is such a bonding thing; but limited for us by the gulf between the huge range of things I like to eat, and what Dave will maybe, possibly eat some of. Can you feel my pain? I started off full of enthusiasm and have somewhat lost my zeal for substituting nuts and lentils for everything with a face (in Dave's world, even prawns have faces; so he doesn't eat them). We have had lots of arguments about it; but four years later, I have accepted that this is just the way it is. And looking back at my own child-hood, I can see that my mother's way wasn't necessarily the best either. She loved us but she never knew where her next penny was coming from, and she worried about us all going hungry; so she wouldn't allow us to be fussy. Dave's childhood was different – not well-off either, but secure and happy with two loving parents. Also he has had asthma all his life, and I suppose that might have made his mother more indulgent with her wee chicken. Anyway, it's just the way it is, and it's a good job that I'm an inventive cook who likes veggies because other-wise we'd have slain each other by now. Having said that, as time goes by, I eat less and less meat and have extended my vegetarian repertoire considerably. And have regained a bit of equilibrium.

Soon after coming to Newburgh I went to a cross-party group on 'Food' at the Scottish Government. I'd been introduced to these public meetings by Christine, my Food Hygiene tutor; and on this particular occasion I met Jon Wilkin and Karen Barton, lecturers at Abertay University in Dundee. They suggested I join their Masters programme in Food and Drink Innovation. I liked the idea and followed this up next day; was accepted and offered a fully-funded place; and started immediately.

I can't describe how brilliant this experience was for me. I wasn't really ready to retire; I wanted to learn more about food and drink to feed my blogging habit and give me a bit more credibility as a food writer; and it was easier to settle in with Dave when we had a bit of space apart. And the Masters programme was really excellent. The tutors were approachable and helpful, the subjects were challenging given my lack of science knowledge, but achievable, and the methods of teaching were fairly hands-on. The other students, mainly in their twenties and many of them from mainland Europe, were a nice bunch with a range of backgrounds, and we all rubbed along nicely together. Travelling there wasn't a problem; I only had to be physically present in Dundee three days a week, and I could drive the ten miles to Cupar, then use my bus pass. It was nothing but good from start to finish.

I had to work very hard, though. There was a definite generation gap between me and the other students when it came to study methods. At the start of each lesson I would dig out my notebook and pencil case while they all fiddled with their phones. Instead of taking notes from the whiteboard, they would take photos. When we had to arrange to meet in small groups for class projects, they arrived late then whizzed through rapid-fire Facebook messaging while I arrived early and sent laborious texts. I have somewhat grudgingly had to learn that those things you carry around called mobile phones aren't really phones at all. They are computers. And my skill in touch-typing doesn't carry over to a keyboard the size of a matchbox.

We studied a range of subjects which would take my student peers on to various careers in the food and drink processing industries. I found some of the subjects easier than others – the absolute hardest, for all of us, was statistics. The ones I loved the best were research-related (apart from stats – pity). And right at the start, I found the module on Professional Development very inspiring because the tutor challenged my overly nervous and self-deprecating presentation of myself. He gave me to understand that this was my own, important, opportunity, and I was to make the best of it (and not make feeble excuses about age). The modules we covered were:

• Professional development

• Clinical nutrition

• New product development

• Packaging and sustainability

• Food hygiene and quality assurance

• Research methods (including the dreaded stats)

• Research project.

If I were to make any criticism of the programme, it would be that sustainability should have had a higher profile – with climate change and political turmoil, widespread food poverty, the oceans drowning in plastic and Scotland's terrible record for obesity and lifestyle-related disease – environmental issues should, in my view, have been at the heart of it all. But maybe that would have made it too hard to cover other core subjects. In any case, I got to explore these issues through my choices of assessment.

The assessments were fairly practical in approach – e.g. we had to write an essay on the impact of the Mediterranean diet on cancer prevention; and to devise, package and present a reduced-sugar food product aimed at primary-school children. I wrote an essay on the challenges to the food industry of making packaging that was accessible to older people; a presentation on food hygiene factors in the industrial production of meat pies; and a research proposal on evaluating the Scottish Government's strategy on food poverty, which entailed a visit to FareShare in Edinburgh, where supermarket surplus was gathered and redistributed to the hungry poor. I volunteered for a placement with Dundee Food Bank, which was sobering. We also had some really interesting company visits – e.g. to Algie's coffee importers and distributors in Glasgow, to a slaughterhouse in Perth, to a potato breeder in Forfar, and to a craft brewery in Dundee.

The Research module took up the entire third semester, with everything else we had studied intended to build into it. We were put into pairs and had to devise and carry out a research project from a limited list of options – current issues in the food and drink industry. Other choices included insect protein as a way of feeding the world; extending fava bean use as a high-fibre option; enzymatic browning and potential cancer risk. All fascinating in their own way.

Chrysa, my research partner, was a talented and gorgeous young Greek student. She and I negotiated a project around making a distilled alcoholic spirit from waste bakery products, with our steeped-in-the-industry supervisor, Professor Graeme Walker. Chrysa's interest was in brewing, mine in addressing food waste, so this proposal met both our aims. A branch of the artisan bakery Fisher & Donaldson in nearby Cupar gave us a ready supply of leftover bread and broken oatcakes, and we were off.

Chrysa did the science bit of the project – brewing and filtering and adding yeast and all the rest of it – and took me to the lab sometimes to see how it was all going. I did the commercialisation investigation, and went round speaking to craft brewers and distillers, artisans and salespeople. It was challenging and absorbing, although for a while I thought my contribution to the project was pitiful. In due course I came to recognise that for all Chrysa's scientific brilliance, and producing a spirit with definite potential, the commercial side was also fundamental; without it, no product would ever achieve life beyond the lab. I learned a huge amount about marketing alcohol, in a very short space of time. Abertay's events and PR people decided our project was newsworthy, and managed to interest Scottish Television in coming in to film us in the sensory lab. So I was on the telly, talking about food waste! What a laugh.

Graduation was on 5th July 2018, and was such fun. Harry came up the day before, and I drove him and Dave to the Tay Bridge for the bus. Dave and I used our bus passes, much to Harry's irritation because he had to pay the full fare of £1.50 (you can take the boy out of Scotland – but can you take Scotland out of the boy?!) Five minutes later we arrived in Dundee. I collected my robe and academic hood, and we went and had a nice light lunch. Then Dave thought it would be a good idea to get some photos outside Braithwaite's, the delightful coffee emporium which I'd often visited on my way back to the bus station to return home. Braithwaite's was founded in 1868 and moved to its present premises in 1932, with the current owner being the fourth generation of his family to put the kettle on. The shop, with all its original fittings, is part of Dave's earliest memories of Dundee. So there we were, Dave, Harry and me, the three of us posing and taking photos of each other, when this flashy car drew up and two bling-laden women jumped out. They were waving warm congratulations to me although I was certain I hadn't met them before. I couldn't quite understand their interest, because only a street away there were hundreds of people milling around in gowns taking photos. One of them offered to take a picture of all three of us; Dave muttered, 'she's pissed,' as I handed over my camera. She took a few pictures and then handed the camera back. 'It's just so lovely,' she gushed, 'to see how you can make something of yourself NO MATTER HOW OLD YOU ARE!' Then she and her friend went merrily on their way, leaving us creasing ourselves laughing. And I have to say that the photos she took were the best we got that day, pissed or sober.

After the ceremony we were greeted by a piper in the square as we came tripping down the Caird Hall steps; it brought a tear to my eye, and I was delighted with my nice thick-paper certificate announcing that I'd earned a Master's Degree in Food and Drink Innovation – with Merit! We got on the bus back across the bridge then Dave took over the driving, and we went to The Newport for a completely delightful dinner, treated by Harry. Jamie Scott, the chef at The Newport, had won Masterchef a few years previously and I'd been lusting after a visit there, but it had always been too expensive. For my special occasion, it was wonderful. All local ingredients, lots of foraged stuff including black garlic, which I'd never come across before, and beautifully presented. Good veggie options for Dave. Local beer, wine and spirits. It was heaven.

COURTSHIP LOAF – AKA MAYA ANGELOU LOAF (SPOT THE ALLUSION BELOW)

If breadmaking is your thing, you can easily do the plaited loaf with which I went a-courting. Use mainly or wholly white flour, a kilo if you want a big one or less – depending on the scale of your courting ambitions!

1kg strong flour, 15g instant yeast, 10g salt, 50g melted butter, 600ml warm water.

Put the flour, yeast and salt in a bowl and mix in the warm water and melted butter. Knead – 10 mins by hand or 5 mins in a stand mixer. Put it in an oiled bowl, cover with a tea towel, and leave it for an hour or so to rise. Turn the dough out of its bowl onto a lightly oiled surface, and knock the air out of it.

After knocking it back, flatten it out, then roll it into as thin a rectangle as you can muster. Leave it for another hour. And still we rise! Envisage two lines down its length, dividing it into long thirds. Spread a little chutney on the middle third, then scatter it with crumbled or grated cheese. It's up to you what kind of cheese and chutney you go for, but

MAKE IT HARD CHEESE RATHER THAN SOFT, AND A CHUTNEY WHICH COMPLEMENTS IT.

DOWN THE OUTER TWO THIRDS, CUT HALF-INCH-WIDE STRIPS AT ANGLES, LIKE A CHEVRON – BOTH SIDES POINTING NORTH, AS IT WERE. THEN, STARTING AT ONE END, FOLD THE STRIPS OVER THE MIDDLE, ALTERNATELY FROM EITHER SIDE, OVER THE FILLING, SO THAT YOU END UP WITH A STUFFED PLAIT. NOT TOO STUFFED.

SWITCH YOUR OVEN ON TO HEAT – YOU WANT IT GOOD AND HOT, AND OVENS VARY A LOT. I GO FOR 220 DEG. LET YOUR LOAF REST WHILE THE OVEN HEATS – IT WILL RISE AGAIN. IF YOU WANT TO YOU CAN BRUSH SOME BEATEN EGG OR MILK ALL OVER TO GIVE IT A BIT OF GLOSS; AND SPRINKLE ON SOME SEEDS TOO. THIS ISN'T ESSENTIAL, BUT IT WILL LOOK ALL THE MORE ALLURING. BAKE FOR ABOUT HALF AN HOUR, OR MORE IF YOU THINK IT NEEDS IT.

REMOVE MAGNIFICENT PLAIT FROM OVEN, COOL A LITTLE, AND PLY YOUR PECULIAR CHARMS AS YOU SERVE! I WISH YOU ALL SUCCESS IN THIS, AND IF S/HE TURNS OUT TO BE A VEGETARIAN, I WISH YOU ALL JOY!

STILL I RISE

You may write me down in history
With your bitter, twisted lies,
You may tread me in the very dirt
But still, like dust, I'll rise.

— MAYA ANGELOU

(She's talking about black women in the United States, with a history of slavery. But her poems lends itself generously to elevating the position of downtrodden people everywhere. And also to bread.)

CHAPTER 15: INTEGRITY VERSUS DESPAIR

Did my late-flowering Masters give me what I wanted? More or less. I hear from my former student colleagues on LinkedIn – they're doing a range of jobs and making their way in the food and drink industry both here and abroad. They probably wouldn't recognise what I do as a valuable use of Masters learning, and they could be right. Perhaps I didn't really need to put myself through all that hard work. But it helped me feel my way, like following a thread in a dark cave, through the food and drink journey to a place where I have the relaxed joy of part-time work and a whole range of foodie interests, and am able to spend half my time writing. I couldn't afford it if I didn't have my little pension from my previous mixed-up 40 years of work. Nobody could call any of this a career plan. But somehow I have fetched up in a happy place.

So here I am, having the time of my life. I'm busy; but the work is all of my own choosing. I'm not very well off financially, but I have enough to get by, with no major outgoings. I have a lovely partner and great friends. I'm a lucky woman. How do I spend my time?

I'm a member of Newburgh Orchard Group, whose *raison-d'etre* is to help people with ancient orchards to look after their apples, plums and pears – originally planted by the monks from the 12th century onwards. Last year I learned how to juice apples, and helped run an Apple Day with blind tastings of home-squeezed apple juices. The community orchard could provide apples for everyone in Newburgh, but sadly some are left to rot. The trick is in the storage, as I'm beginning to learn.

I'm a part-time tour guide at the recently opened Lindores Abbey Distillery – the earliest-known location of distilling in Scotland, beautifully restored, and producing a most palatable Aqua Vitae while we wait for our spirits to mature. Being a tour guide is essentially a storytelling job, so it suits me very well. We have visitors from all over the world, many of whom are extremely well-versed in how to make whisky but who just love to visit the places and hear the stories. And of course, sample the wares. Staff training, this last year, has included perching on a bar stool to nose a range of new-make spirits, trying to figure out what sort of cask they have been stored in. I can scarce believe my luck. All that research I did for my first attempt at a novel, about eighteen years ago now, has come into its own. Why, I ask myself, didn't I look for a job in the whisky world long before this? My job isn't well paid but it's tremendously satisfying. Such massive differences in flavour from apparently tiny changes in process or storage. It's utterly absorbing. I also produce the staff newsletter for the distillery, so I get to poke my nose in and ask questions and interview people – it's a job with my name all over it.

Occasionally, for my friend Amanda, I do a healthy cooking demonstration and supper at Maggie's Centre in Dundee. Amanda is a skin nurse, hence also a cancer nurse, and she runs a little support group once a month. Via Maggie's, people with cancer diagnoses can access some really helpful professional support to help them live well with cancer. When I was doing my Masters, I had the opportunity to sit in on a four-session programme at Maggie's, with a retired dietician, who demonstrated how to adjust your diet to give yourself the best chance of a good recovery. I'm not qualified to offer specific recommendations to people, and I don't try to. And I'm always mindful of the things I read about the Mediterranean diet, and the value of conviviality. So, a diet high in fruit and veg, high in fibre, low in sugar and saturated fats, regular oily fish, and with small amounts of lean meat, is very beneficial for all of us. I keep my demonstrations general and simple. We cook around an island unit then share the results, and people seem to enjoy it. It's relaxing and stimulating, and while people are trying something different, they can chat if they wish about the specific issues that are troubling them. It's a privilege to be allowed to join them in their tricky journey.

I'm a judge for the Scottish Craft Butcher Awards, meeting two or three times a year to decide on awards for various butcher products (very welcome in a veggie-oriented home life). In Scottish butchers' shop windows, you will see posters proclaiming that this establishment won a silver, gold or even diamond award for its sausages, or haggis, or steak pies or whatever, in a given year. So the judging I do is the mechanism by which the butchers' goods are graded. A panel of judges – people either in different parts of the industry, or in related fields, or retired from same – are invited two or three times a year to come and do half a day's tasting and judging. It's really very pleasant, and sometimes quite surprising. Obviously, it's great for a butcher's business to be able to claim gold or whatever award status for their goods; but sometimes they also use these competitions to try out something new, and get adjudicators' feedback. 'Sausages' covers a wide field and there is always a good range of pork, beef, chilli, garlic and other spices presented. Last time, though, one butcher with an eye on the gin boom entered the Gin and Tonic Sausage. Weird. I'm a big fan of a nice G&T, but in sausages? Let me just say, it split the judges. The spooky thing was, the sausage tasted just like gin and tonic, which is no doubt a clever thing for a butcher to do. So, some judges felt this should be applauded. For me, it just felt wrong. Wrong. And even more wrong was the White Chocolate and Raspberry Sausage. Yes, honestly. Utterly, utterly, wrong.

Butchers are living through difficult times, with recognition of the need to cut down on saturated fat in our diets, and further research recognising the risks posed by nitrates – a commonly-used form of preservative. Animal welfare is always an issue for those of us who eat meat, and we can't, indeed mustn't, take it for granted that all animals are well cared for. A number of high-profile campaigns have challenged this, and I am satisfied that on the whole, UK and Scottish standards are fairly high. During my Masters programme, I visited a large abattoir not far from home, and felt the system was all right. If anything shocked me, it was the volume of meat passing through. All those carcases swinging by their heels from the overhead pulleys – it was like being in a meaty forest. Amazing how much meat we go through, and we obviously need to cut this down in order to free up land for a more balanced cultivation of cereals and veggies as well as livestock; and to combat global warming.

It's a personal choice, but I believe that if a cow or sheep or hen or pig or whatever has been well treated in life, and killed gently, then this is acceptable. I don't eat very much meat nowadays, and try to ensure that what I do eat comes from reputable sources; and, generally speaking, that it has been produced in the UK. This also takes care of food miles; so although there's probably nothing wrong with, for example, New Zealand lamb, I don't buy it because why would we waste fuel transporting an animal halfway round the world when we can produce our own high-quality lamb at home? Always, the arguments that convince me in relation to food production are the ones which give us our best shot at feeding the entire population a healthy diet. I get very irritated by the kind of Scottish food and drink writing which goes on about our fabulous meat and game and seafood and so on, as if we all lived on scallops and fillet steak. What about people on benefits or low wages, who have to choose between spending their meagre pennies on fuel or food? Or school shoes for the children? The thriving of food banks is a disgrace of the developed world. We simply shouldn't need them in a civilised, wealthy society. Adequate nutrition is a right, not a privilege. Our skilled butchers have an important role to play in all of this, even if times have changed.

I'm not much of a gardener, but lots of people in our small town are very green-fingered, including my friend Judith who keeps me going with courgettes and cucumbers and kale and whatever else is burgeoning forth in her verdant patch. I give her a hand with weeding and she shows me how to do things with my own patch. Judith asked me to help her set up an open gardens day locally, which we have called 'The Hidden Gardens of Newburgh' and it was a major success in its first year, bringing in nearly £2,000 – 60% of which went to our local chosen charity, the Cubs. Over the winter, Judith and I with another friend Paul have set up a little informal group which we call 'The Kailyard' – for people who grow fruit and veg in their gardens and want to share their growing and cooking ideas. It's inspirational. I doubt if I'll ever be a great gardener – my idea of a perfect day in the garden is sitting with my feet up and my nose in a book – but hopefully a little of the know-how will rub off.

In our little garden we have room for one apple tree, some rhubarb and garlic and herbs, and a polythene 'station' on a frame for growing tomatoes; otherwise it's kind of decorative, with Dave's skills and imagination well-deployed in the renovating of old bikes for displaying plants.

I have a lovely little kitchen with lots of time for experimenting; and a loft with good writing space, which I share with Dave's ever-expanding collection of guitars, ukuleles and musical memorabilia. Domestic life is very rewarding.

I have various other writing projects, including one inspired by our group 'Book2Film'. Once every six weeks or so for the last five years, six of us from my Dunfermline days have met to watch a film based on a short story – which we have read in advance of the meeting. It's a rich way to consider the telling of a story – how the different media approach the same material. It's also a great way to keep in touch with old friends, since I and others have moved house during that time, and it would be all too easy to lose touch. One of the successes of our group is the supper arrangements – we had all been in reading groups which poured more energy into competitive catering than into consideration of the book in question. We decided that we would always have a baked-potato meal, with the host for the evening doing the potatoes, and everyone else bringing along something to put alongside them – hummus, cheese, salads or whatever. Pam always does a pudding – except for when it's her turn to host/do the potatoes, and on those occasions I do the pud. So it's always fresh and easy and enjoyable; and for those who don't cook, or don't have time, it's also easy to buy some hummus or whatever, and there's no sense of one-upmanship. This leaves us free to get on with discussing the story and watching the film. You'd be amazed at the number of well-known films which started life as a short story rather than a novel ('Rear Window'; 'Breakfast at Tiffany's'; 'The Third Man'; 'Brokeback Mountain' for instance – and that's just some of the better-known ones.)

Immediately after handing in my final dissertation for the Masters project, I started writing this food memoir; and completed the first draft three months later. It felt self-indulgent – for my own pleasure only – surely, I felt, this book would not be marketable, since no-one would be interested in reading a book by a complete nobody. But then a competition was announced by the Scottish Association of Writers – the first

15,000 words of a minimum 30,000 word non-fiction project. It would be judged by a literary consultant and editor; and hence I thought, even if I didn't win anything, I would get some useful adjudication notes. So I edited my first 15,000 words and sent them in – and won second prize. The adjudicator said that she could see this being a commercial proposition, and so I have trundled on to bring this book to publication. Thank you for reading it.

Erik Erikson, in his famous 'eight ages of man', considers that the final stage of life is all about looking back on one's previous life and finding a sense of either integrity or despair. I have certainly had my periods of despair; and of course I'm nowhere near (fingers crossed) the final stage of my life. Integrity is something to strive for, and take peace in. I have always been interested in food and drink; and find myself deeply favoured in all kinds of foodie ways, even if I can't afford to eat out in fancy restaurants. Everyone has a right to eat a healthy diet but across the world, most people can't afford to; and others choose not to. My own bumbling attempts to understand food have brought me great joy. I wish I could find a way of feeding the world but till I do I'll just keep on eating, drinking, cooking, feeding, reading and writing. Here's to all of you who are doing likewise. Let's collaborate.

BABETTE'S FEAST

The Danish author of the short story 'Babette's Feast' was Isak Dinesen. Her story was made into a film in 1987 and features a dwindling and austere Protestant community in a remote part of Jutland, in the 19th Century. Two elderly sisters preside over their father's legacy – a strict and plain-living body of ageing believers, following a rigid code. One day a French woman, Babette, calls with a note of introduction from an old friend – she is a refugee and needs work, and a roof over her head. So the sisters take her in, and Babette cooks for them. They are a little disapproving of her little extravagances but feel it would be disrespectful to complain.

One day, Babette wins the French lottery and decides, in her gratitude for being given a home, to spend her entire winnings on a magnificent meal for the church community. The members are all shocked and horrified at the expense, but decide that to be polite, they will eat the meal without commenting on it. There is to be no sinful relishing of extravagantly rich ingredients; no crass displays of enjoyment; but they do not want to rudely refuse.

You really need to either read the story or watch the film to

ENJOY THE OUTCOME – I DON'T WANT TO SPOIL IT FOR YOU. BUT BRIEFLY I WILL SAY THAT THE INEVITABLE HAPPENS, AND THE CHURCH MEMBERS ARE ENTICED AGAINST THEIR BETTER JUDGEMENT. THEY COME TO RECOGNISE THE LOVE AND SACRIFICE IN BABETTE'S GIFT, AND TO SEE IN IT A FORETASTE OF HEAVEN.

IT'S A BEAUTIFUL STORY. I WISH I COULD COOK LIKE BABETTE BUT SINCE I CAN'T, I WILL HONE MY SKILLS AND TRY TO BE GENEROUS. BIG THANK YOUS TO ISAK DINESEN, THE AUTHOR OF THE STORY; AND TO GABRIEL AXEL, WHO DIRECTED THE FILM.

NO SPECIAL RECIPES HERE – WHATEVER YOU COOK, JUST LAY IT OUT WITH KINDNESS.

POSTSCRIPT – SAUSAGE SANDWICHES REVISITED

At the start of this book I explained my earliest food memory, and expressed a wish to feed the world, especially those families with fathers who didn't do the right thing by them. During my lifetime, since my father's tentative but (perhaps undeservedly) successful peace-offering, I have witnessed a renaissance in sausages – maybe two words you wouldn't expect to find in the same sentence. Dismissed for a long time as cheap and nasty, there has been a renewed interest among craft butchers in producing a high-quality, tasty product – as evidenced by my meat judging experiences.

Recently I was asked to lay on a children's buffet for a church event, and I tried to steer a line between keeping it healthy and making sure it would be enjoyable. I look back on Cabbage Wars with my own mother, and Minach and Bourgettes with Harry, and recognise we were unusual. So many children these days seem to be unbearably fussy, and wedded to stuff like chicken nuggets which bear no resemblance to any kind of happy hen. But there's no point in producing a buffet which no-one will want to eat. So I devised this, which went down well:

The Enormous Crocodile by Roald Dahl ('Roald Dahl's Revolting

Recipes') – two baguettes laid end-to-end and filled with egg mayo, its front end wedged open like jaws, a big pink tongue made of ham, almonds jammed in as teeth, and adorned with spinach and boiled-egg eyes to make it look like a crocodile – very fetching!

Macaroni Peas (Hugh Fearnley Whittingstall) – sauce made with more peas than cheese, some of them whizzed in the blender

Leek and Cheese Quiche

Lots of salady things, hummus and dips, fruit

And a huge pile of sausages! Easy to oven-cook in large quantities in the oven, and very tasty

Home baking provided by the Mums.

How do you get children (or adults) to try something different? Gentle persuasion. How do you eat an elephant? One forkful at a time. How do you feed the world? Answers on a postcard please.

LAST WORD ON SAUSAGE (or other) SANDWICHES

Terry Wogan (1938–2016, an Irish TV presenter on BBC), gave a recipe for the book 'Food Aid', which he jointly edited with Delia Smith, on how to feed the world:

'Take two slices of bread. Put a fiver in between. Post to Africa.'

...or words to that effect.

BIBLIOGRAPHY

Dahl, Roald. 'Revolting Recipes'

Dickson Wright, Clarissa. 'Spilling the Beans'

Earl Hammer, Jr. 'The Waltons' – television series first shown September 1972, based on his book 'Spencer's Mountain'

Eastwood, Clint. Director of film 'Invictus', 2009

Greene, Graham. 'The Third Man'

Henderson, Fergus. 'Nose to Tail Eating: A Kind of British Cooking'

Henley, W.E. 'Invictus' – poem first published in his 1888 'Book of Verses'

MacKie, Christine. 'Trade Winds: A Caribbean Cookery Book'

Milne, A.A. 'When We Were Very Young'

Morton, James. 'Brilliant Bread'

Munro, Neil. 'The Vital Spark'

NAAFI (Navy, Army and Air Force Institutes) Cookbook 1939 –

sadly out of print and unobtainable unless like me, you have inherited a copy. There are however lots of new books available which emulate the 2WW rationing 'experiment'.

Patten, Margeurite. 'Perfect Cookery'

Reed, Carol. Director of 'The Third Man' (film, 1949)

Reiner, Rob. Director of 'When Harry Met Sally' (film, adapted from Nora Ephron's book)

Sekules, Veronika. 'Friends of the Earth Cookbook'

Smith, Delia. 'Delia's Complete Cookery Course', first published 1982, still in print

Smith, Delia and Wogan, Terry. 'Food Aid Cookery Book', 1986

Whitehorn, Katharine. 'Cooking in a Bedsitter'

Whittingstall, Hugh Fearnley. 'The River Cottage Meat Book'

Zola, Emile. 'Germinal'

ACKNOWLEDGMENTS

My nearest and dearest have been very supportive in helping me get this book ready for publication; and many friends have taken a substantial role in inspiring or correcting or suggesting the content. I'm grateful to you all.

Specifically, I'd like to say a big thank you to Dave Burnett for putting up with me and giving me breakfast in bed; and for telling people I was a writer before I really believed it. To Harry Welsh for sending me 'Invictus' when I was at the limits of my courage – and for so many other things. To Marian Weir for being the inspiring friend who took me to France and opened my eyes to another world. And to Claire Wingfield for suggesting that this book might be worth completing.

A couple of people who have 'gone before' have been immensely influential and I would like to light a virtual candle in memory of Grace Mitchell – thank you for the meringues and tattie scones, and for being a friend; and most of all, to my mother Jean Bruce McCulloch, for all her fortitude and good humour through my first 21 years. Despite the sago.

IF YOU LIKED THIS BOOK, YOU MIGHT LIKE MY NEXT ONE TOO.

'Book to Film: Great Adaptations' tells the story of B2F, our film group. Since November 2013, six of us have been meeting to discuss a short story or novella which we have all previously read; and then to watch the film adaptation. We meet in each other's homes and take along contributions for a simple supper; and with great enjoyment and a bit of argy-bargying we have reached the 50 mark, six years later.

It's a winning formula. Sometimes we think the book is better than the film, and sometimes the other way round. More often, some of us prefer the book and the others, the film. Occasionally none of us like either, or we all like both. But always, always, even if we've hated both the book and the film, we have loved the process of examining them together. Book groups across the world have learned the added value of shared discussion around a book; we've taken it a stage further.

I have referred to the book and film 'Babette's Feast' within the pages of 'A Life in Mouthfuls'. This was one of our finds, and gives a sample of what's coming up in the next book. To pre-order your copy, please visit www.hlwelsh.co.uk and contact me. I look forward to hearing from you.